D0528846

Dalai Lama, My Son

DALAI LAMA, MY SON

A MOTHER'S STORY

Diki Tsering

Edited and Introduced by
Khedroob Thondup

This book is dedicated to the people of Tibet, who are still suffering under Chinese rule. It is also dedicated to the memory of my sister, Yangzom Doma, who gathered all these stories, and to the memory of my mother, who so encouraged my sister to initiate this project.

This paperback edition first published in 2001 by
Virgin Publishing Ltd
Thames Wharf Studios
Rainville Road
London
W6 9HA

First published in Great Britain in 2000 by Virgin
Publishing Ltd

First published in the USA in 2000 by Viking Penguin,
an imprint of Penguin USA

A catalogue record for this book is available from the British Library.

ISBN 0 7535 0571 1

Typeset by Intype London Ltd
Printed and bound in Great Britain by Mackays of Chatham PLC

Contents

II. Mother of Compassion

Acknowledgements

I would like to thank my literary agent, Eileen Cope, Rinchen Dharlo from the Tibet Fund, Janet Goldstein of Viking Penguin and, of course, Holly Hammond, who shaped the book.

Introduction

*M*y first memory of my grandmother was when I was seven years old. It was 1959, and I was attending St Joseph's College, a Jesuit school in Darjeeling, India. One day the rector of the school, Father Stanford, called me in to his office. 'Young man,' he said, 'today history is being made. Your parents have asked for you to go home, for you are to go to the train station at Siliguri and receive His Holiness the Dalai Lama, who will be passing through that area.' That was my first inkling that my family was special.

When we arrived at the station, we had to make our way through crowds of people who had gathered to pay their respects and get a glimpse of His Holiness, who had recently escaped from Tibet and found refuge in India. I knew then that I was part of something important. My uncle, whom I had not yet met, was being received as a living Buddha. The people were calling my grandmother Gyayum Chenmo,

Great Mother, and she carried herself with the dignity and warmth befitting the name.

After coming to India, Mola, as we called her, first lived with His Holiness in Mussoorie. (*Momo* means 'grandmother', and *la* is an honorific.) Then she came to live with us in Darjeeling. She adapted to life in India with the calm and patience that had sustained her through so much upheaval. Her purpose was always clear: the care and guidance of her children and grandchildren. Through war, hardship, illness, death, and in spite of the inconveniences of politics and national borders, she was the rock to which her family was moored. She was the harbour where safety and love could always be found.

Grandmother was easy-going and kind, but she was very particular about the upbringing of all her grandchildren. She insisted that we eat properly – that is, foods native to Amdo, where she learned to cook from her own mother. We all learned to cook from her. She often prepared meals and baked breads for His Holiness, but she also taught his attendants – people from central Tibet – to make Amdo cuisine. To this day the fourteenth Dalai Lama eats the same dishes that his mother made for him when he was a child.

Grandmother was also the keeper of religious traditions and festivals. At New Year it is customary to wear your best new clothes. When I was very young I loved to wear the brocade *chubas* that Mola would send us from Tibet. But after 1959, when refugees were flocking to India with no money and no possessions, she told us not to wear our fancy clothes at New Year, out of consideration for those people who had nothing. We had to wear one small article that was new, but not to show off our finery.

My father, Gyalo Thondup, had become head of the family after his father died. He played a major role in engineering His Holiness's escape from Tibet. Grandmother told me that, after my father, it was up to me to carry the family name, and she impressed upon me the significance of that responsibility. These are traditions that I now pass on to my daughter. They might seem like small things, but I believe they are the values that form a strong character.

The care and attention she lavished on her family naturally extended to all people – friends, government officials and ordinary people. If she saw poor Tibetans outside the window in the street, she would call out to them to come up to the house. She would look at their faces and say, 'You look sad. What's the problem?' They would usually say they had no money, and on the spot she would put some cash into their hands.

Early every morning many people would line up at our back door to ask for food. We kept huge boxes of rice and wheat, and we gave each person a scoop for the day. Those early years in India were hard, and Mola did her best to help people.

An American government official lived next door to us in those days. I happened to see him again in 1979 in the States, and he spoke of my grandmother. When his wife gave birth to their first child, he recalled, Mola prepared chicken soup and sent it over for the new mother – in the first month after childbirth it is considered very important for the mother to take good care of her health. This man never forgot her generous gesture towards someone she hardly knew.

Everyone respected my grandmother because she didn't put herself above or below anyone. She treated each person she met with consideration. Even the people who worked in her household loved her. Instead of sitting back and giving orders, she would join in the task at hand and show the servants how to do it.

Grandmother was a pious lady. She would say her prayers first thing each morning and make offerings to the family deity. She taught us the rudiments of religion by her example. I used to keep aquariums, and I fed the fish with live worms. When Grandmother saw me doing this, she was horrified and told me it was very sinful to let one living being eat another. That had a great effect on me, so after that we switched to dry fish food, so we wouldn't have to take part in any killing.

She loved the fish. We watched them together and gave them names. She would point out the different characters of each fish – which were mean and which were gentle. She gave us an appreciation for life.

From March to November we were away at boarding school. Then the whole family would go to Calcutta for the winter holidays. Mola was in her sixties, but she was open to everything and liked to have fun. She would take us for picnics and to sample Indian snacks on the street. She loved to see films, and she often took us with her. She especially loved Indian films with singing and crying and lots of emotion. They were in Hindi, of course, so she couldn't understand the dialogue, but we would fill her in on the plot. She herself was a great storyteller. She liked to scare us with stories about the cat ghost that would steal bread from a rich family and give it to a poor family. Her son Norbu had gone to the States to teach at the University of Indiana. When she visited him there, she liked to watch late-night horror films on TV.

Whenever my brother and I were having a fight, Mola would break it up and decide who was right and who was wrong. We respected her decisions, because she was always fair. She never imposed anything on us, nor would she ask us to do anything for her. Her warmth and affection gave us a great sense of security.

She had huge cupboards where she kept her belongings. She kept them very neat, with everything in its place. Deep in some drawer or shelf of these vast treasuries there would always be sweets or a treat of some kind for us grandchildren. Whenever we wanted something we asked her for it, because she was always ready to give us whatever she had.

I admired my grandmother's strength, both physical and mental. We built a new farmhouse with steps leading down to the yard. One day she slipped and fell down this flight of eight or ten stairs. We all rushed to see what had happened. There she was lying on the ground. She was an elderly lady, and she had hurt her back. But in a moment she got up and said, 'I'm fine'. Her reaction to pain was minimal. She was seldom sick, and she kept very fit. Many of her children died in infancy, but she withstood this suffering with composure and self-control.

Grandmother had worked hard most of her life and didn't like being idle. When she lived in Lhasa and was pregnant, she used to go up on the roof of the house and carry stones back and forth for exercise. Just as people lift weights nowadays, she would carry stones. She always told us, 'You people are really spoiled. You don't know how to do hard work.'

In the early 1960s we set up an Office of Tibet in Geneva, Switzerland, and His Holiness's brother Lobsang Samten went to live there as our representative. My grandmother went and spent some time with him and his family. After that she went to Bloomington, Indiana, and stayed with Norbu's family for a while. She visited each of her children in turn, including His Holiness at Dharamsala and us in Darjeeling. All of us were happy to see her because we enjoyed her company. She never scolded or criticised anyone. Her natural authority commanded respect.

My father had left Tibet for China when he was only sixteen. He wanted to get an education and learn the ways of the government. While he was there he married a Chinese woman, and because there were strong anti-Chinese sentiments among the Tibetans, my grandmother advised my father not to return to Lhasa with his wife. Instead he and my mother went to live in India. There in 1950 my sister was born, in 1952 I was born and in 1954 my brother was born.

My grandmother was very open and accepting towards my mother. In spite of the age-old suspicion and rivalry between Tibetans and Chinese, the two of them got along very well. Mola had sent her own youngest daughter and her grandchildren to school in India, where my mother looked after them. Even though my mother, as a modern, educated woman, managed her home and raised her children in ways unfamiliar to my grandmother, Mola recognised what my mother was doing, and gave her full support. She saw that my mother could look after six children, treat them as her own, and make them think progressively. I never heard a word of criticism or anger between them, nor did I ever feel the slightest bit of resentment on either side.

My mother was also a great lady, from a famous Chinese family. Her father had been a general under Chiang Kai-shek. She had gone to college and was preparing to go to the States to further her education when she met and married my father. She proved herself not only as a good wife and mother but also as a dedicated public servant.

In 1959, when the refugees started coming to India, my mother thought it was important for them to become self-sufficient. With the proceeds from a benefit football match, she was able to buy a piece of land from the Jesuits, and she built a self-help centre. My mother worked hard there every day, and by the time of her death in 1986, nearly six hundred people were living and working at the centre.

After my sister, Yangzom Doma, finished college, she went to England to the School of Oriental and African Studies in London, where she did graduate work in Chinese and Tibetan studies. When she came back to India, my father suggested that she go to work for the Tibetan government-in-exile. He always encouraged us to fulfil our duty to our people and our country. My sister took a job at the Library of Tibetan Works and Archives, where she became editor of the *Tibet Journal*.

While Yangzom Doma was in Dharamsala she would frequently visit Mola who, of course, would cook my sister's favourite foods. One day in 1979, my sister came up with the idea of recording our grandmother's life history. When she proposed the idea, Mola was taken aback. Nobody had ever asked her what she felt or thought about the events of her life. But she agreed to tell what she could remember, and over the following year or so they talked, and Yangzom Doma scribbled notes. Once Mola started reminiscing, she needed very little prompting. She took to the task with such enthusiasm, my sister told me, that the stories seemed fresh even after many decades.

Tragically, my sister was killed in a car accident in Tunisia in 1982. The news reached me first, and I told my mother. She collapsed in grief and never really recovered from the shock of losing her only daughter. She developed cancer and died in 1986. Thousands of Tibetans gathered to say prayers for her when she died. Even though she was Chinese, people revered her.

I got married in 1983, and my wife soon became pregnant. One night in a hotel in New York City my sister appeared to me in a dream. She told me that my wife was going to have a girl, and that she was going to be that daughter. I didn't tell anybody because I didn't know whether to believe it or not. When my daughter was born, my mother was really happy. It brought a little joy into her life after my sister's death.

I got divorced when my daughter was five, and have brought her up for the last eleven years. I have to say that she resembles my sister in many ways. Her handwriting is just the same, for instance. I have kept all my sister's clothing and effects in boxes in our attic, and my daughter loves to go through them. She says, 'How strange that Yangzom Doma had all these things that I like.' She likes to wear all my sister's clothes. Now I'm convinced that my sister has been reborn in our family, and that makes me very happy.

I made a promise to my daughter that, as long as she was young, I would not remarry, but would devote myself to her upbringing. We've become good friends. But last year I told her, 'You've got your own life now. I'm 48, and I need someone to accompany me into old age. I want to get married.' She agreed. I recently remarried, and my wife and I had a baby daughter last June. We gave her my mother's name. So now I think that my mother too has been reborn into the family.

When my mother died, the people at the refugee centre that she ran went to see His Holiness to ask him to appoint me to look after it. I said I would do it if my brother, who is a doctor, would help me. So that is what we have been doing from 1986 until today. The centre occupies 90 per cent of my time now.

The centre is the most progressive one in India because it doesn't rely on charity. We make carpets, we have a state-of-the-art printing press, an X-ray clinic, a blood lab, a hospital and a school. We serve 750 people. To support my family I go off to my farm in Kalimpong at weekends where I have a noodle factory. My noodles do well in that area. I am also an elected member of the Tibetan Parliament. I do travel a lot and speak for Tibet especially when I am in New York, Washington D.C. and Japan.

Because my sister died before she was able to complete this book, it fell to me to carry on this important project. My grandmother spoke only Tibetan, and my sister translated her stories into English. I compiled the notes for publication. Although the story recounted here is incomplete, it is an important reflection of the life and times of Diki Tsering and a tribute to the efforts of my sister. I am pleased that a wider audience can now get to know my grandmother. This account does not do justice to her.

I.

Daughter of Peasants

1

Looking Back

I have had a strange, almost unreal life, now that I try to recollect my history. You must forgive me if my memory lapses occasionally. It is all so very long ago, and my childhood has never been a conversation piece until today! I don't know how to be interesting. It's amusing that you ask me the date of my birth. If I had ever asked my grandmother such a question I would have been severely rebuked for showing such disrespect. How times have changed!

Honestly, I do not know the exact date of my birth. What relevance did dates have to us? We were born without much fanfare, matured into adolescence, were married, had children ourselves, and then were overtaken by death. We lived the entire cycle simply, in the belief that people are ordinary and that existence is natural.

I was born approximately in the first month of the Iron Ox year (1901). I was named Sonam Tsomo. My birth name belongs to another life. Most people know me as Diki Tsering, but I was not born Diki Tsering. Ever since I went to live in Lhasa, I have tried to become Diki Tsering, with all the social forms and graces that go with that name. Because of the responsibilities I owed towards my new position in life, I gradually eased out of being Sonam Tsomo, the simple girl with her simple life and the ordinary ambition of being a good housewife and mother. I feel very tender towards the young girl that I have forced myself to forget.

It was both faith and fate that propelled me into the unbelievable life as the mother of the Dalai Lama. When it happened, it seemed as if I lost all my courage and confidence, and I became afraid, like a little child, at the formidable task that lay before me. But once I began to tell myself that I was Diki Tsering, the name given to me on my wedding day and means 'ocean of luck', a kind of rebirth kindled all the forces of determination within me. I was no longer afraid, and I willingly challenged fate, determined not to be submerged by the tide.

Today I am a tiresome old woman, my body feverish with rheumatism. But however debilitated you become physically, the spirit of youth is constant and alive. It never deserts you, even in the face of the greatest suffering. My only companions now are memory and reverie. My mind goes back more and more to my childhood, my parents and grandparents, my birthplace. I see so clearly the meadows, the stream, the hills, the farm where I grew up, and I feel so strongly the cycle of returning home on this last lap of my journey.

Traditions are so easily broken and forgotten. Today when I see young people, I often think that they are reacting against their traditions in order to over-emphasise their modernity. I am proud to be, despite my resilience and ability to change, a very traditional woman. Does this make me archaic and anachronistic? I don't think so. I have always been proud and strong-willed. I have fought many battles, and have emerged stronger after each victory. My traditions, my roots as a Tibetan, have fortified me. Traditions cannot be denied or forgotten. They are the creators of your spirit and your pride and the backbone of your sensibilities. They make you what you are and define what you want to be.

2

My Earliest Years

A few days before my birth, my grandfather paid a visit to a local lama, insistent that his forthcoming grandchild was going to be a girl. 'I feel it in my bones,' he declared. 'She is going to be someone. Please help me find a name for a very special girl who is going to be a very special woman.' A few prayers and many hours of astrological consultation later, the name Sonam Tsomo was decided on: *Sonam* meaning 'fertility', *Tsomo* for the great goddess of longevity.

In our traditional, peasant society, religion was our sole justification for existence. It brought serenity, peace of mind and contentment of heart. Religion – I call it faith – was part of every aspect of our daily lives. The priest, representing God on earth, was invited to participate in all the major events in the cycle of life – birth, marriage, travel, illness, death and afterlife.

My earliest memories are of a land that nature had made a plentiful paradise. It was a wealth of forests, lakes, hills, mountains and fertile soil. This is how I remember the village of Churkha, in the district of Tsongkha, where I was born. Churkha was under the jurisdiction of Kumbum monastery. Tsongkha was the birthplace of Tsongkhapa, founder of the Gelugpa sect of Buddhism in the fourteenth century. I was the second child born to my parents, but the eldest girl. Perhaps my birth was considered a misfortune to my parents, for it heralded a long line of girls in my family.

I have never forgotten the freedom of my young days in Amdo (one of the two Eastern provinces of Tibet). I grew up with seven sisters and three brothers, surrounded by great affection and friendship. My parents were humble but prosperous peasants, and my horizons and my awareness began and ended with the lives of my forefathers, tillers of the soil. That soil was the means by which we earned our survival and existence. When fate changed my life so swiftly and abruptly, I was but a peasant girl.

My early years were spent within a large extended family. My father had six brothers and they all lived in our household with their wives and children. This custom was peculiar to our area in Amdo. Sons brought their wives home to their families of birth, while daughters left their home upon marriage and joined their husband's family. Sometimes, when parents had only daughters, they 'acquired' a bridegroom to enter their family to continue the family name, but that was not typical.

The houses in Amdo were different from

those of central Tibet. They were square, with either one or two floors. Our home was double-storeyed, and we also had a single-storeyed house where the servants lived. The houses were made of *thala*, two wooden walls filled with pounded sand. Village houses were surrounded by a stone wall and were built around an inner courtyard. An extended family would often live in a cluster of such houses. Every house had a large store room for *tsampa* (roasted barley flour, the staple food of Tibet), flour, butter, dry meat and oil. The stables were separate, and here we kept the sheep, cows and horses, *dris* (female yaks), donkeys, pigs and *dzomos* (the off-spring of a yak and a cow – the male is called a *dzo*).

In our area we had the fiercest-looking mastiffs that I have ever seen, even in Lhasa. They were used as guard dogs. It is known that these dogs were often exchanged for horses. They often had to walk great distances when they were traded, and they would develop sore paws. We would wrap the sore paws with yak fur as padding.

My father was called Tashi Dhondup and my mother was Doma Yangzom. My grandparents also lived with us. In Amdo all the older women in the family were called *amala*, or 'mother'. To distinguish between the various mothers, we would use terms like *tama* and *gama*, elder mother and younger mother, in accordance with their seniority. It was customary, as a mark of filial devotion, that those of the older generation who had grown-up children did not work. It was thought that the old folks had done their labour during their youth.

From the moment of my birth I was loved by my grandparents, not because I was the eldest – I already had an elder brother – but because some premonition told them that I was to be a special child and an even more special adult. They lavished such tenderness and affection upon me that I felt cherished. The enjoyment of life that resulted has never left me. To them I owe eternal gratitude for enriching my childhood and for hiding from me, however temporarily, the fact that a woman's life can be hard, cruel and full of trials and tribulations.

My grandparents formed the nexus of my entire world. I slept with them, ate with them, was cajoled and petted by them. They seemed to fill up my entire little self. This was possible because of the unrestrained and informal relations between grandparents and their grandchildren, which lacked rigid rules of conduct.

My grandfather was a strong, imperious, slightly arrogant man. At that time in Amdo it was the grandfather who was lord, and he ruled with an iron fist. This tempestuous man cradled me in his arms the instant I was born and declared loudly, 'She is my Sonam Tsomo.' With this sweeping statement, I became his charge. Even if they were needled by this dominance, this exploitation of authority, my parents could do nothing but obey.

It often seemed strange to see my parents defer to my grandparents on every matter of consequence, and yet give in to every caprice and whim of mine. It was only much later that I came to understand the respect underlying our kinship ties, and how it marked every aspect of our behaviour. Grandparents were regarded by all members of their family with awe and respect. Yet the relationship between grandparent and grandchild was marked by casual intimacy. Parent–child relationships were restrained, distant and very formal. My own parents' relationship with my grandparents was like this.

I would notice, often with secret glee, how awestruck my parents were by my grandparents. For instance, if my grandfather was sitting on the *kang* [a heated platform used for sitting and sleeping], my father was socially forbidden to sit beside him. Out of deference for his elder, he had to either stand or sit on the floor. But I could crawl up on the *kang* beside my grandfather and feel the security of his arms around me. I would deliberately provoke my father in this way, to show that in the presence of my grandfather I was the little mistress of all and could do as I pleased.

When my grandfather was having tea, his favourite drink, convention forbade my father to drink tea unless my grandfather ordered him with 'Tashi Dhondup, sit down and have a cup of tea.' Even then, my father would never draw up a chair, but had to be content to squat on the floor. Chairs were only for equals meeting each other eye to eye.

Every evening after sunset, when the family got together for a meal, I would edge close to my grandfather – a secret sign between the two of us that we were going to have a marvellous time after the meal. I would listen spellbound as he told countless legends and stories. My favourite was the one in which he overpowered all opposition in the final selection of my name. My grandfather was the main influence in my life in those early years. He knew how to enjoy himself and taste fully every experience of life.

Even when I was still quite little, the fact that I was a girl weighed heavily on my heart. From very early in life, we were aware of the different roles and aspirations of males and females and the preference families had for sons. The birth of girls was sometimes looked upon as a curse. I heard a story about a poor family who drowned a female child immediately after her birth. Daughters were viewed as an economic liability in our farming society. As a child a daughter consumed without contributing to the production of food. Then, as a teenager, she had to be provided with a dowry, whereupon she left her family to marry and join her husband's family. Sons, on the other hand, increased production by their labour. They remained with their families, and their offspring increased the family wealth even more.

Many a time I would ask my grandfather whether he would have preferred a boy. I would not have been able to bear the disappointment had he affirmed my fears. But he would tweak my ears and say, 'Would I have said you were a girl even before you were born?' Then I would be transported by great joy. It meant a great deal to me to be wanted for myself and not for the practicality of my sex.

Those early years were so full of every kind of pleasure that I have never forgotten them. I had the freedom to laugh as if I had heard the funniest joke in the world, to see the beauty of the trees and the flowers, to feel the contentment of the horses and cows and to dream every dream that my little mind could call up.

3

A Carefree Childhood

The separation from my grandparents came unexpectedly. In 1905 my grandfather bought a farm in Guyahu (also called Tanantwan), about 75 km from Tsongkha. This was originally a Muslim area, and after the Muslims waged war with the Chinese, they were expelled. It was then that my grandfather bought this property. Upon his return to Tsongkha, he informed his sons of his purchase and asked whether one of them would like to go and live in this new place. My father's two brothers were reluctant to go on the grounds that they did not want to live in a Muslim area. My parents therefore offered to go.

I do not remember my family moving because I was only five. As far as I can recall, it pleased me to move to my new home because it was a novel experience and I would be seeing a new place. Although I was fond of the place of my birth, I felt not a twinge of regret. It was still a time when I could play and not have any responsibility.

Guyahu was a lovely place, not much different from Churkha. The distance between the two was not very far; we could travel between the two places in three to five hours on horseback. Transportation in those days was solely on horseback and on carts drawn by *dris*, *dzo* or horses. We moved to Guyahu with eight or nine servants, one goat herd and a few people to tend the animals, taking with us only clothes, food and basic necessities.

It was heartbreaking for me to be separated from my grandparents, but my grandfather would come and visit us frequently. He loved horses, and took every opportunity to ride out to visit friends and relatives. On parting he would tell my mother, 'Doma Yangzom, don't let the children go out, but let them remain in the terrace or in the garden, or else the wolves will eat them.' Wolves were known to carry away children. Anyway, since we were girls, we were rarely let out of the house except to the terrace. My parents were very strict with us.

Relationships among brothers and sisters were tender and warm, with brothers often assuming the role of 'little father'. The bond between brother and sister was particularly tender, with an underlying current of sadness, because the sister would soon get married and leave home. It was also a brother's duty to give his sister a lively and emancipated childhood, so she could carry her dreams with her into adulthood.

I had three brothers. The eldest remained at home with his wife and children. Another died when he was ten years old. When my third brother was born, my parents went to the lama and asked for his advice about whether their son should be a monk or a layman. The lama advised my parents to send him to the monastery. If he were kept at home, they were told, he would not have a very long life. People have great faith in the lama, so it was decided that my younger brother would go to the monastery at Kumbum.

I was deeply attached to this brother. Because I was aware that he would soon leave us to become a monk, I would give him more affection and love than I gave the others. In fact, when I saw any of my other brothers or sisters quarrelling with him, I would immediately rush to his defence and begin a fight on his behalf. When he did leave home, my parents and I went frequently to see him, and often he would come back for visits.

In most Tibetan families, one son was sent to the monastery, unless the family was small with few sons. In that case the boys were required to work on the farm. Boys were generally sent to the monastery by poor families, because maintaining a boy economically and eventually supporting his family entailed burdensome expenses. In Tsongkha it was unheard of to send girls to become nuns, nor was there any nunnery nearby. In Lhasa, many girls were sent to the nunnery, some for economic reasons, as parents found the burden of securing marriages for them too demanding.

After we moved, my carefree childhood came to an end and my life entered a new phase.

There was now no time for play. I became the charge of my mother, who began to teach me about the world of women and train me in household duties in preparation for marriage. In Amdo at that time many of the household responsibilities fell on the shoulders of daughters, even when they were quite young by Western standards – six or seven years old. I had to learn to make noodles, brew tea and bake bread for the entire family. At age seven I could scarcely reach the top of the cooking table, so I would have to stand on a chair to prepare the dough.

At the back of our house was a courtyard-cum-garden with a high, thick wall. When my parents went to the farm, I was put there with instructions to prepare the lunch. They would leave, bolting the door of the house from the outside. We were trained from a young age to dust and sweep our rooms. If we didn't clean thoroughly, my mother would say sarcastically, 'Why are you cleaning up like a cat washing his face?'

When I was not cooking or cleaning, my mother would teach me to cut out clothes and do embroidery. It was considered disgraceful for women in Amdo to not be able to embroider our native dresses and boots. By the time I was twelve, I was making my own trousers and blouses and those of my brothers and sisters.

My mother was extremely good at stitching. Upon the marriages of all her eight daughters, my mother stitched their trousseaus without any assistance. No one employed a tailor. No matter how many family members there were or how many clothes, boots and hats were to be sewn, it was all done within the family.

This was the education for girls in 1907. At the time it was unheard of for girls to go to school, to learn to read and write. Boys had to till the land and work on the farm from a young age. If the family was well off, and there were many sons, the sons would be sent to school. The school was rather far from the place where we lived in Tsongkha, so my brothers were not sent to school. The schools taught students Tibetan, Amdo, Chinese and the Tsongkha dialects. My father had had a basic education for four years and knew how to read and write.

Our only other training was in prayer. In the evenings, when we lived with my grandparents, my grandfather would summon us for daily prayer sessions. Even when we moved, our prayer sessions continued. We would gather together and recite the rosary for an hour or two. My grandmother prayed every morning at the family altar, after lighting butter lamps and making offerings to the gods. Then she would walk in the courtyard, saying prayers on her rosary. If we were working in the fields and saw a lama, we would immediately prostrate ourselves on the ground three times. As peasants we didn't have much understanding of religion, but we had great faith.

4

Life on the Farm

Our farm was in a beautiful place of level land with plentiful trees and lakes, hills and mountains. The land was very fertile, and any crops grown would have a good yield. We fertilised with manure. We would cut the grass and mix it thoroughly with earth, turning it for a few days. We would burn it until it had a reddish tint, then grind it and mix it with coarse cow and goat manure. This manure, when dried, was also used as fuel for the *kang*.

The *kang* was a raised platform that filled the entire room, and all of us would sleep on it. Family members would even have their meals together on it. The structure was made of clay brick and was hollow. We would fill it with dry grass or sand and dried manure or wood, then light the fire. On the surface of the *kang* we would place a carpet and over that our bed clothes. We would keep adding wood and dried manure to the *kang* fire, keeping it burning throughout the day. It was so cold that despite the *kang*, we still had to cover up with heavy furs. Without the *kang*, I think we all would have frozen to death.

In the summer months the weather was very warm and pleasant, with temperatures between 80 and 90°F. But in the winter months, from the tenth month onward, the weather was very cold indeed. It was so cold that if we left any tea in our cups overnight, the next morning the tea would have frozen and the cups would have cracked. It was so cold that I have heard of people walking for short distances and their feet falling off as a result of frostbite. As much as ten feet of snow would fall sometimes, which came up almost to the second floor of our house. After a snowfall it would take us about two days to clear the snow.

Since nothing could grow in winter, we stored our potatoes, radishes and other vegetables below the ground. We dug a cellar about ten feet deep and twenty feet wide, with steps leading down, where we would stack all of our essential commodities. The lid to this cellar had to be sealed firmly, or everything would freeze.

The farm was large, so it was impossible for us to do all the work. We had to hire outside labour, which could be classified into different groups. The *nyohog* were employed on a monthly basis, and the *yuleg* worked for us on a yearly basis. From the second month to the fourth or fifth month, there was a lot of work on the farm. In the fourth month the cutting of hay began, in order to store fodder for the winter. In the seventh month we sowed *tema*, or peas. We had many farm hands until the tenth or eleventh month, after which the yearly workers would sow barley. We grew wheat, barley, peas and mustard. In fact, we grew almost everything that could be cultivated there. All this was more than enough for home consumption, and we sold the surplus.

My father used to have his breakfast, and then pick vegetables from the garden and distribute them among his neighbours by throwing them over the fence surrounding our garden, especially to those who had no vegetable gardens of their own. Neighbours were very close to each other. Whenever we had free time we would go up to the roof terrace and converse with our neighbours. My father would often invite his friends and relatives over for meals and wine-drinking sessions, and he would not let them leave until a few days had passed. He was very fond of drinking.

After the age of fifty, my father did no work; my elder brother supervised the farm, and my father would occasionally take a tour of it. My mother would cater to the household's needs. Even to the age of seventy, she was still very active and would do her embroidery. Her eyesight was very good.

We had no watches to tell the time. We were guided by the sun and the sky. We would place a stick in the earth, and if the shadow fell upright this indicated that it was midday. If the shadow was a little inclined, this indicated that it was past midday. By nightfall the shadow was almost level with the ground. At night we would look to the stars as a guide.

I had many friends to play with as a child, mostly neighbours. Toys for children did not exist, so little girls would gather together and play at household duties. We would cut up pieces of material and sew them. We would also find scraps of paper and draw whatever was in sight, such as flowers and houses. I also loved to build little castles in the sand.

When I was about twelve or thirteen, my father showed me where he hid his money. After the servants and my brothers had gone to the fields, my father would take me to the stables, where he would unearth his money, which he kept in large earthenware vases. I would assist in the unearthing and the replenishment of the vases, which we would then seal and put back, covering them with mud. I loved this secrecy.

5

Amdo Society

*C*lass distinctions were marked in Amdo[1] at that time. Those in the servant class, for instance, remained in the kitchen, and there was no social intermingling with them, even in the household. Those on the lowest rung of the social ladder were robbers and thieves. Next came the butchers and those who came into contact with leather and furs. When we had to employ butchers, hospitality dictated that we should give them a cup of tea. But after they left we would wash their cups in ash, a ritual that was supposed to sterilise the cup. In Lhasa craftsmen who worked silver and gold were also considered inferior, and were not even permitted to enter the house. But the most socially inferior people, so low they were not

[1] Amdo is on the frontier with China, and its borders have long been in dispute. Although it was populated mainly by Tibetans, the Chinese claimed it, calling it Chinghai. Since the eighteenth century its kings and warlords have often been supported by the Chinese government. During Diki Tsering's early life, the area was ruled by Ma Pu-fang, a Chinese Muslim warlord who was supported by the Chinese Republicans.

even on the ladder, were the corpse bearers – those who took the dead to their final destination.

Lamas – the spiritual masters – were in a class by themselves. They were given great respect and placed foremost in the ranks of society. As peasant folk we were deeply religious, although not in an intellectual way. Lama robes implied for us the robes of Je Rinpoche, which was our name for Tsongkhapa, the great upholder of the Buddhist faith, who came from Tsongkha. [Rinpoche is an honorific title for lamas who are reincarnations of great teachers; it means 'precious one'.] Even the poorest of clerics was honoured by hospitality in our homes. This was not the case in Lhasa, but in Amdo if we met a lama on the road, we would immediately invite him to our house and entertain him with the best food and the best tea, served on the best crockery.

The wealthy families had large farms and servants, but economic wealth was fairly evenly distributed, and real poverty was nonexistent. We did not have any *miser*, or bonded labourers, but servants were hired. In our village there were about a hundred families, each cultivating a piece of land that they owned. We did have to pay a certain amount of taxation to the Chinese government, whose local governor was known as Ma Pu-fang.

Most of the people were farmers, but we also had our merchant class. These were a mobile people who carried boxes of wares with them and would come to the villages to sell matches, soap, thread, wool and other basic necessities.

Generally money was not used; things were bought with barley, wheat and other such items of exchange.

There were also many little shops in town selling basic necessities, like tea and cloth. When we bought things we paid with barley or other farm produce. There were restaurants and roadside inns, as well. I remember the delicious aromas coming from these restaurants filling the air.

6

Foods of Home

Kitchens were the pride of every housewife. They were very large, with walls constructed of stone. The cooking surface was a long stone, sometimes as long as eight to ten feet, with five to eight cooking holes in it. Through a large hole in the side, the stove was then filled with dried goat manure as fuel, and the fuel would be lit through this hole. Every evening three large containers of fuel were put in. The next morning we would bake one of our traditional breads, called *kunguntze.*

Bread was an important part of our diet. We also made *timomo*, or steamed dumplings, in six bamboo steamers, piled one on top of the other. Another type of bread, called *kansho*, was baked in the oven by putting dry white sand in the stove, then putting wood over the sand. Once the sand and wood became red, we would place the dough in the fire. Bread baked in this fashion was so delicious and never, ever got burnt; it always came out golden brown. Another type of bread, called *kuki*, was baked in an earthenware vessel, left over the fire for about two hours. This bread was reddish, due to the addition of turmeric powder, and contained molasses and walnuts.

Our days were not easy. Housewives did all the cooking for family members as well as for the employees. All the female members of the household would help. In the morning we gave the servants *timomo* and *tsampa* with tea. Sometimes we gave them porridge with milk and salt. In Tsongkha we had something called *yenmi*, a crispy bread, dry-baked in sand, ash and manure or wood. We had to make more than a hundred of these on the days we ate this bread.

Lunch was taken to the workers in the fields. Sixty layers of *timomo* – about 1500–2000 dumplings would be steamed. In the evening we gave them noodles and soup, cooked in a huge pot that could hold about three hundred bowls. We never used pans or utensils made of aluminium or tin; if we did we were called beggars. We used pots made of iron or clay.

In our native place we had many types of *tsampa*, made from barley, oats and peas. When the weather was very cold, *tsampa* was our main staple. Sometimes we would give the servants a type of *tsampa* cooked in oil. They appreciated it that way, because they did not become hungry so soon after eating. They burned a lot of energy working in the fields.

Typical Amdo dishes, called *ranfan* and *chowtuan*, were made exclusively from barley. The barley had to be cooked in a little water and stirred vigorously until it became a thick paste. Nowhere else in Tibet was this dish eaten.

Meat was eaten only twice a week. We would make a stew with thirty to forty pounds of meat. At New Year we would hire a butcher to come and kill the pigs. It was considered a sin to do it ourselves. Sometimes yaks and sheep were also butchered. We then dried the meat by hanging it in a special room upstairs.

As a child I found it very exciting when the women of the household prepared our native noodles, for which Amdo is famous. In summer we ate cold noodles, *thukpa*, and in winter we ate noodles cooked in soup. The highlight of the preparations for me was to go into the courtyard behind the house to grind garlic and chilies for the noodles. No one could hear the noise I made there, so I would go undetected long past my bedtime. My grandfather would scold me affectionately, saying, 'Look at you, you are smelling of garlic. What will the others say?'

7

Dialects and Dress

There are numerous dialects in Amdo. Because we came from Tsongkha, we spoke the Tsongkha dialect, though my parents were also acquainted with the Amdo dialect. There is a great deal of difference between the two. In Tsongkha, since there were many Chinese there, the younger generations would converse in Chinese and often would forget their native Amdo. In Guyahu the older people would use Amdo; the younger people spoke Chinese. There was no overlap between Chinese and our Amdo dialect. Though we could understand a stray word or two, Chinese sounded like a person speaking incorrect Tibetan.

After the Muslims left our area, the population was mostly Amdos and Chinese, with some tribal people – nomads who tended yaks and made cheese and butter. I still remember the differences between us, particularly in styles of dress. We Amdos would wear our traditional *hari* (a vase-shaped head-dress studded with jewels, reaching to the waist). The Chinese wore something called *baochidue,* a woollen cloth covering the back of their heads. They would tie up their hair in the *dzachiba* style – a pointed knot at the nape of the neck, decorated with horse hair. This was further decorated with silver and gold ornaments, depending on wealth and social class. They also wore the *jalung* and the *tungduntze,* which were similar to the *hari,* made of cloth and attached to the braids of the hair.

I have heard it said that Amdo borrowed many of its customs from China, particularly in styles of dress, but I don't think this is true. The Chinese wore long robes, belted and with buttons, but the Amdo women wore the traditional Tibetan dress, or *chuba,* which I still wear today in India. In winter our dresses were lined with fur and heavily padded with cotton. On the lower edge was a border of various colours – white, red, yellow and green – and below this was a border of otter's fur. In our area women never wore the traditional aprons, or *pangdens,* worn by the ladies of Lhasa.

Jewellery was compulsory for adult women. We had to wear rings on all ten fingers. Our ears were pierced with two holes in each ear, one above the other. The lower hole was for the earring, about five inches in length, while the upper hole was for a smaller adornment. But the most important jewellery was the *hari.* After I was married, I used to wear a *lenpai hari,* which had everything included in it, and also a *tangyo,* which was a belt attached to the *hari.* In addition to this we wore the *jalong,* which was two flaps of cloth to tie the hair from the waist to the floor, decorated with silver, turquoise and coral. We also wore a *rawang*, a kind of cloak with two narrow flaps on either side and a broad flap in the centre. All these items of dress were for married women only.

On rising in the morning, we immediately put on the *hari*. Without it, we were not allowed to enter our shrine room for prayer. A woman was not permitted to remove her *hari* in the presence of any elder, not even her father-in-law or mother-in-law. In fact, a married woman was not permitted to wear any hat in the presence of her in-laws, not even a handkerchief on her head, no matter how strong the sun, as it would indicate disrespect. Even when women were working in the fields, they were not allowed to cover their heads. If young people were in the fields with no elder present, then they could place handkerchiefs on their heads. These handkerchiefs were made from denim, folded into quarters, and the braids of hair were tied around the handkerchief.

Both men and women kept long, braided hair. When they were working, it was practical to wind the braids around the head. But the instant any elders would come by, the braids were whipped off and allowed to hang down their backs, as a mark of respect.

Women's hair was braided into about seventy tiny plaits. After a hair wash it would take us the entire day to decorate and to do our hair into braids. On either side of the head we made about fifty braids, and at the back of the head about twenty broader ones. We would wash our hair every week, and the braids would be done until the next head bath. If we had a lot of work, the braids would not be redone for a month.

The boots we wore were different from the normal *sombas* worn by other Tibetan women. Our boots were called *yohai*. They were elaborately embroidered and tied up at the knee. The sole of the boot was made from hemp covered with cloth, about two inches thick. We made the soles ourselves. The upper portion of the boots could be made from brocade, silk, or other material, over which we did embroidery. As we were peasants, we went about barefoot in the summer. In fact if we wore shoes then, we were called 'grandmothers' by the elderly in the village.

When I was young my clothes were about the same as for the adults, except for the *hari*. Little girls had five braids in their hair – two small braids at the side and three at the back of the head. The belts of our dresses were placed a little above the waist.

8

Traditional Festivals

he largest festival of the year was the Tibetan New Year, or Losar. Elaborate preparations were undertaken for Losar, beginning after the eighth day of the twelfth month. For twenty days we made noodles, pastries, rolls, *kabse*, and *timomo*. We would allow these foods to freeze naturally and stacked them up in the storehouse until they were required.

Bread was now baked for the first, second and third months. It was then stacked in rows and allowed to freeze. The evening before we wanted to eat the bread, we would place it in a container and heat it a little. If we forgot, there would be no bread to eat the next day, as it would be hard as a rock.

On the eve of New Year, we would cook a pig's head and boil some mutton and pork. (We did not eat chicken or fish.) Then we would invite all our friends and relatives to have dinner, consisting of noodles and meat. No one slept on New Year's eve. We drank wine and amused ourselves all night. I used to be so happy on this day, as were all the other children, so excited that it was Losar. I would repeatedly enquire, 'Has the sun risen? Has the sun risen?', for that was the sign for the festivities to begin.

We would go out in our newest and finest clothes, and on our horses we would put the most elaborate bridles and saddles. We would set off firecrackers and guns, and sing and shout '*Lha gyal lo*', a festive cry that means 'Victory to the gods'. We would visit all our friends and give gifts, which consisted mainly of bread and pastries. As children, we had to prostrate ourselves on Losar, touching our heads and bodies to the ground three times in the presence of our parents, grandparents and all the elders. Then we would present our gifts of bread and greet each other with '*Tashi deleg*', 'Good fortune'. If lamas were nearby, we would all go for blessings.

On the second day of Losar, we would go for a day's pilgrimage to visit sacred places of worship. Until the fifteenth day everyone had a good time. Men played mahjong and dice, the young people sang and danced, and the children played games, including *sham-liu*, or swinging. After the fifteenth day of the first month, the elderly and those who didn't work continued the fun, while the young people and the servants resumed work. After the second day of Losar in Lhasa, the entire city remained orderly and calm because of Monlam, or the Great Prayer Festival, which begins at that time. In Amdo we did not have such a custom.

The next festival arrived on the second day of

the second month. This was the day we brought our horses to the horse fair. Horses were bought and sold here, and there were horse races. This festival was exclusive to Tsongkha and did not occur in other parts of Tibet.

There was a festival on the eighth day of the fourth month, when a lot of strange things happened. Oracles would go into a trance and give predictions. Couples who were barren would say certain prayers, and as part of a ritual they would fetch water in a bucket thirty to fifty times, saying repeatedly that they wanted a child.

The fifth day of the fifth month was wine-drinking day.

On the sixth day of the sixth month everyone went for a picnic to an area with mineral springs that we considered very good for the health. The springs there were good for the stomach, the eyes, the hair and the feet. There were 108 of these springs up on a hill. The girls and women went in one party, while the men and boys went in another. They even took different food. Once both parties arrived at the springs, the food was exchanged and songs were sung to each other. These songs could only be sung in the hills on this day and not in the home. A whole day would be spent in this way, under multicoloured umbrellas. How happy we were in those days, with not a care or worry.

On the fifteenth day of the eighth month, pastries known as *yubin*, or moon cakes, were exchanged among friends and relatives. Between six and seven in the evening we placed the cakes decoratively on trays, together with an assortment of fruit, and placed them under the moon as offerings. Then we lit butter lamps to the gods and prostrated ourselves three times to the moon. Afterwards we could eat the fruit and cakes. Some of us as children would slip quietly past the trays and, when no one was looking, load our pockets with the delicacies.

During the Mongol supremacy in China, the rulers were greatly disliked by the people, and secret organisations were formed. One year, on the eve of the moon festival, an uprising took place against the Mongols. Letters and messages had been placed within certain cakes, and the uprising was organised in this way.

The twenty-ninth day of the ninth month was tanners' day, the fur and leather sellers' day. There is a god associated with this festival, and offerings were made to him so that the weather would change and become cold, and people would come and buy furs.

In the tenth month there was a day to invite monks to come and say prayers in your house and offer butter lamps. In the evening we would go to the nearby monastery and take oil to light the butter lamps. Since the monks were saying prayers in each of the homes in the neighbour-hood, families would take turns preparing food for them. In the evening all the children would take their bowls and go to the place where the prayers were being conducted. There they would find a large pot filled with noodles. It was compulsory for each child to help himself to one bowl. From another pot all the grown-ups would have to partake of their share. This festival continued for eight days.

On the ninth day of the eleventh month we had to save the life of a horse and a sheep from the butcher and say prayers for three days. Then we sent the animals to the monks. Bread was baked and sent to the monks at Kumbum, and they said prayers for us.

9

Haunted by Ghosts

When I was young I loved to listen to stories, as all children do. We would gather around my grandfather and listen to folk tales. Even grown-ups would attend my grandfather's storytelling sessions. There was such an intimate atmosphere. The women would do their sewing and knitting, and we children would be so excited. I inherited the knack for storytelling from my grandfather, and after my marriage I would often conduct storytelling sessions for my children and my neighbours' children.

As village folk we believed in ghosts and superstition. Most of us had encountered ghosts first hand. There was a ghost called a *kyirong*, which could emerge in a variety of forms: as a boy, a girl or a furry cat. I encountered this ghost numerous times, and it caused me great suffering and fear on four occasions.

Once, when I was gravely ill, the *kyirong* appeared to me in the form of a little girl. She brought me a large bowl of Chinese tea and struck me lightly on the head. I had been lying in bed, and the moment she struck me I woke up, due to the loud sound, though I felt no pain. She then invited me to drink the Chinese tea, which I refused. When I tried to rise from the bed, I noticed that the bowl contained blood. With that she slipped to the door, laughing all the while, and disappeared.

In Tsongkha there was a household that maintained a *kyirong* on a permanent basis. This was a well-to-do family, but no one would give their daughters in marriage to this family, due to this ghost. No matter how beautiful or intelligent their daughters were, they never had suitors, because people were afraid of them. The head of this family finally made a whip from the wool of a sheep and brandished it about in his house saying, 'If you are black or white, show yourself immediately. It is all on account of you that my children have no husbands or wives.' This caused the *kyirong* great panic, and he was unable to remain in that household. Only after this did those children contract marriages. I have heard that this same ghost would waylay people on the roadside and tell them that they had no idea what it was like to be without freedom. He said he was filled with nostalgia for his home.

The *kyirong* made its mark in Lhasa, too. We had bought a good steed from the household where this *kyirong* lived and brought it with us to Lhasa. Certain acquaintances met the *kyirong*, who told them that he had come along with the horse to Lhasa. At that time I had a dream in which a man entered our stables, and when he left he was riding on our horse, which was ill at the time. When I told my husband this dream, he said that the horse would definitely die. By nightfall the horse was dead.

The *kyirong* was really a nasty character. If he did not like you, he would turn your house upside down and take all your furniture and cooking utensils out into the garden. In the kitchen he would upset everything in sight. Huge sacks full of peas and flour would be upturned and havoc would ensue. This ghost would hear and understand whatever we said to him. He would answer in giggles and laughter. He would steal anything to eat, but he never stole money.

On one occasion my daughter and I were having tea, and I told her to fetch the leftover roast mutton. When she went to the larder, the mutton had disappeared – the *kyirong* had taken it. Sometimes when we had made dumplings, the top layers of the steamer would be full, but the lower layers would be empty.

In my native place the *kyirong* was maintained in a neighbour's household. He begged the owner of the house to keep him, and in return he would bring the owner whatever he desired. Once a Muslim cobbler came to stay there for ten days to make shoes and boots. The cobbler noticed that there was a room that was always locked. Nobody went in or came out of this room, but from inside a roaring sound could be heard, as if a person were sound asleep and snoring. The cobbler immediately knew that the *kyirong* was in this room. One day his master went out to the fields, and the cobbler unbolted the door of the room to have a look. To his horror there was a cat the size of a tiger with long white whiskers, sleeping in a prone position, just like a human being.

I once had a maidservant whose aunt, after many years of marriage, gave birth to a son. One night she discovered her baby dead – his neck had been twisted. Later the *kyirong* told people that he killed the baby due to jealousy of the parents' affection for the child.

The deaths of four of my children were due to this ghost. After the birth of my son Norbu, I had two sons who both died. [Norbu was Diki Tsering's second child, born in 1922.] Ten days after the birth of one son, he fell ill with a severe eye infection. His eyes swelled up, and he could not open them even to feed. At night when I was resting beside him, I heard heavy footsteps echoing on the ceiling. The footsteps descended to the window, and then the door unlatched itself and the *kyirong* came and stood beside me. Out of fear, I quickly lit a few oil lamps. I took my newborn infant and placed him on my lap, thinking that the ghost would not be able to harm the child if I had him in my grasp. The lamps gradually flickered lower and lower, until I was left in the dark and could no longer see anything. I lost all sense of reality and time. After a while I heard the sound of a child crying in the distance. Opening my eyes, I realised to my horror that my child was ten feet away, on the floor, crying. The lamps were once more lit, and I was still sitting upright. I was not aware how my child had got to the floor.

For about fourteen days after that, my son was severely ill, his eyes swollen out of proportion. He cried constantly, and nothing I could do would comfort him. In the mornings I would notice bloody scratch marks in and around his eyes, and there were bloodstains on his cheeks. Three weeks later his crying ceased, but he seemed lifeless. When he could finally open his eyes, to my horror his eyes had turned from brown to blue. He had become blind.

Some time later this ghost came to us again, this time in the form of an old man. After his visit my son's eyes became swollen again. My eldest daughter's eyes were also affected and swollen. She then grew a growth in her eye, which remained with her until her death. This time my son's illness was fatal. He was just over a year old when he died.

Soon after that I gave birth to another boy. This boy was the joy of our hearts. He was bright and lively, but for some reason the neighbourhood children were afraid of him. If they wanted to play around our house, they would first enquire whether this son was around. If he was there, they would run away and hide. He was very active, always around my skirts, begging for sweets. Unfortunately the *kyirong* struck this little son of ours. He suddenly developed diarrhoea, for unknown reasons. He was sick for one night and died immediately. He was eighteen months of age.

On the night he died my husband's aunt

dreamed that a stranger visited us, and on his departure he was carrying away our little boy on his back. She understood immediately that some unfortunate incident had taken place. The *kyirong* was the most frightening experience of my life.

10

Getting Married

During childhood, despite the fact that I had a lot of chores and work, I was extremely happy. But after I got married, at the age of sixteen, I had a most difficult time. But I'm a Buddhist by upbringing, and it is our belief that in order to live a full and self-contained life, it is imperative to suffer. Thus you can grow and develop not merely into an adult, but into a being who is fully human. It was this basic creed that saved us women, especially, from despair and hopelessness. This faith saved me from the death of my spirit during the first few hard years of my marriage. Without this strength, I would have succumbed to a bereft existence.

As girls we were taught that our only future and hope was marriage and a life of hard work. We led a rigorous life, which was bare in the extreme, with no entertainment or amusements. On some occasions there were folk dramas, but even here we had to be chaperoned by our parents. We were never permitted out alone. Once we had passed the age of puberty, if there were guests in the house we had to stay in our rooms, doing our work. We were never permitted to mingle with the guests, even out of curiosity. It was considered bad manners even to look at visitors.

Marriages were always arranged. In Amdo terminology we referred to this as *longchang*, or 'begging for a bride'. A spokesman would be sent to ask the grandfather's consent; parental approval was not so important. Then we had to ask the *ngagpa*, a priest and also our astrologer, whether it was auspicious for such a marriage to take place. If he decided that it was, after doing a *thudam*, or divination, and referring to the horoscopes of the two parties concerned, then the marriage would be agreed upon. The astrologer was a lama, and his words were always taken seriously. When I was young, I had many suitors, but whenever my family went to the *ngagpa*, he always rejected the marriage, saying that it was not suitable.

Marriages were contracted between two bodies of kin as a kind of alliance, and were settled when we were very young, about eight or ten years of age. Marriages could even be decided when children were one or two years of age, or between two women friends, even when the children were still in the mothers' wombs, on the condition that one mother had a girl and the other a boy. When a girl reached the age of fifteen or sixteen, the man would ask for her in marriage, saying that someone was needed to look after his home.

In considering a betrothal, great stress was placed on economic position as well as on other factors, such as the personal character of the family, particularly the girl's mother. It was thought that if the mother was good, then the daughter would be good. In Amdo the people were all hard-working and placed great importance on honesty. In enquiring about a family, one would ask, 'Are the bones clean?' Families generally aspired to marry into a family of higher rank than their own. But if a poor family had an intelligent son, he was considered a favourable match. Relatives were never permitted to contract marriages with each other, no matter how distant the relationship.

My husband's parents did a *thudam* for him at a monastery when he was quite young. The lama's verdict was that it was propitious for him to become a monk; otherwise he would die quite young. (How strange that this verdict coincided with his actual life, for he did die relatively young!) My husband's parents went against the wishes of the *thudam* and persuaded their son to take a bride, to which he consented, because there was no assistant at home to help his aged parents.

I was recommended to my husband's family through a neighbour who was acquainted with them. They approached my grandparents, who did a *thudam*. The reply was favourable, saying that at the outset the marriage would be difficult but later it would be very favourable. My grandmother was pleased with the offer of marriage. She said that among all her many grandchildren she knew me well, and she would like me to marry into Taktser Rinpoche's family, as it was well known as a good family. She had seen two of the daughters at Kumbum during a festival, and they both seemed very intelligent and well brought up.

In this way it was decided that I was to be married to Taktser Rinpoche's nephew. When the proposal first came, I was thirteen. The go-between who brought the proposal was an old man, who came with ceremonial scarves and gifts for us – hair ribbons, material for dresses and brocade for belt ornaments – as was the custom. He also brought each of us a mug of *chang*, barley beer. This little ceremony indicated mutual consent by both sides in the forthcoming marriage.

My reaction to all this was a firm 'no'. I told my parents that I did not want to get married, that I wanted to stay at home and look after my grandmother. When I was quite young an astrologer had told my grandfather that I should never be sent away from the family, as I was such a good girl. If my grandfather sent me away in marriage, then ill-luck would befall the family. But my parents rejected the views of the astrologer, on the grounds that they had sons and their wives to be maintained at home, and that it was economically impossible to keep a daughter and her husband in the house too. My grandparents and parents informed me that they had consented to my marriage and that I would be leaving home, just as my younger sister had done before me. I tried to insist that I did not want to get married, but to no avail. My grandmother joked that if I remained at home, I would soon 'fly over their heads', meaning I would take over the household. Today a girl would go against her parents' wishes if she did not want to marry the man chosen for her, but in my day we girls were too naïve.

In preparation for my marriage, clothes and shoes had to be made as well as earrings and rings, as part of my trousseau. A girl's wedding in those days was not a simple matter – 35 pairs of shoes had to be made, and 32 sets of clothing. For three years my mother hand-stitched my clothes, shoes and other necessities to take away with me, besides attending to all the other household chores. I had great admiration for my mother's handiwork; she was an exceptional seamstress and embroiderer. From the head-dress to even the soles of my boots, my mother did everything by herself. As she completed each item, she would fold it neatly and place it in a trunk. She would not let anyone else touch the clothes she had made. It was considered to be extremely bad luck if a pregnant woman touched any of a bride's trousseau. If this happened, purification rituals had to be done.

When I was fourteen my future husband's father came to us and asked that I be given in marriage immediately, as they were now old and would like someone at home to look after them, and would like to see their son settled down. Their two daughters had brought their husbands into their household, because there was a shortage of sons in the family. But these sons-in-law never stayed home and were even hostile towards the parents. The daughters therefore were very unhappy, and this affected the performance of their household duties. But my parents told them that I was still too young and did not know anything about housework, and that I could be married when I was sixteen.

Marriage plans had to be finalised through a go-between, a party to the groom's family. Upon his arrival at the bride's house, his hat was snatched away, and a bucket of water was thrown over him. On his hat a radish, fried bread and two sheep's tails would be stitched with thick, coloured thread. All the women would lie in wait for him at the door, their long sleeves filled with *tsampa*. While singing and dancing they would throw the *tsampa* in his face. They would some times rub ash and oil all over his clothes and face. This pretence at antagonism signified the family's sadness and reluctance to part with their daughter.

There had to be a few months' interval between the betrothal and marriage. The interval between my engagement and marriage was two months. Preparations for the marriage took place during this interval by the relatives of my mother and father. During this festive period, a variety of foods were made, wine was drunk and all of our neighbours, friends and acquaintances were invited to partake of the preparations, accompanied by songs.

I was married in the eleventh month of 1917. This date was fixed by the astrologer after reading our horoscopes. We had a lot of prayers said as a plea to the gods that no harm should befall the bride and her party during the wedding journey.

Just before the marriage, my in-laws present-ed me with about twenty items of clothing – dresses, shoes and *haris*. It was customary for the bride to wear the bridegroom's family's clothes when she left her natal home. My in-laws also sent the horse for me to ride on. If the groom's family was well-to-do, they would make certain prescribed gifts. The father-in-law would give a good horse, and the mother-in-law would give a *dzomo* (a female *dzo*) to the bride's mother, so she would have milk to drink. Elaborate brocade was placed over the *dzomo*, and ceremonial scarves over the horse.

On the evening before the wedding, my hair was washed and made up by a girl whose birth horoscope was in harmony with mine. I was born in the Iron Ox year, so the girl who washed and did my hair had to be born in the Dog, Bird, or Ox year. At this time all the women kin knot-ted my hair with black thread and refused to let my *hari* be tied, weeping all the while in a show of grief. I was not permitted to come into con-tact with pregnant women or widows.

The guests arrived early the next morning and were entertained all day with parties. The next day I departed for the groom's house. The hour of departure had to be worked out by the astrologer. I left at six in the morning. Four or five women arrived to escort me, and they had to be able to sing. I dressed for my journey and waited for the women on the *kang*. When they arrived, I stood up and the women sang to me, 'You must dress well, wear your belt properly, or else in the future, no matter how hard you try, you will never be able to wear your belt properly. If your dress is crooked, then your dress will always be crooked.' All the women, including myself, wept throughout the singing.

The escorts then told me to say farewell to my family and our personal deity. All these commands were done in song. I went to the altar room, where I prostrated myself three times. Then I did the same thing in the kitchen. I went to the courtyard, where prayer flags flew from a long pole. I went around this pole three times, after which I mounted a horse. I was given a red woollen shawl with which to cover myself, so that no one could see my face and hands. I was not permitted to look around me, and sat crouched low on the horse. Then, with two women on either side of me singing, we set off for the bridegroom's house.

My father and my brother accompanied me to the groom's home. My mother and other family members had to remain at home. When I was leaving, my father repeated in a sort of wail, 'Sonam Tsomo, *yong wa chi*', which means 'Sonam Tsomo, come home'. Meanwhile, my mother took all the clothes that I had worn on the previous day and burned them in the stove. She wailed into the stove, calling my name in anguish. Both of these customs indicate sorrow at the parting from their daughter.

All the guests on horseback and in their finery witnessed my departure. I took with me clothes, hats and boots for the bridegroom, clothes for his mother, and shoes and gifts for his father. If the groom had important relatives, each of them would also receive clothes. Distant relatives got scarves. If there were many gifts to present, then many people would come along to assist the bride – twenty or thirty people would be included in the bridal party or, if the family was rich, fifty or sixty. Everyone sang songs along the way.

Midway to the groom's house – a journey of six hours – the women singers returned home, and I was accompanied the rest of the way by two older women. When the party was about to arrive at the groom's residence, the groom's party came to receive us. They raced their horses and playfully pulled off each other's hats. Then they offered my party tea, a well-brewed soup and steamed bread. But I got something different: sweet rice, steamed with dates.

When I was about to arrive at the groom's house, an old man, known as *janggu* ('a man to lead'), was sent to meet us. Still some distance from the groom's house my party dismounted and walked beside me, holding the bridle of my horse and singing songs. At the doorway, monks were saying prayers, and the astrologer determined where I should dismount – north, south, east or west. The astrologer washed my female companions in milk. In the meantime I had covered my face with the backs of my hands. I was not permitted to let anyone see me, nor was I permitted to look at anyone. On my forehead I wore a three-inch brocade sash, decorated with silver, to which tassels were attached to block my view.

When my party arrived, the groom's party came out and offered ceremonial dialogue in poetic form. A ceremonial scarf was handed to the groom, and he rode his horse up to the entrance of the house. He then brought out a dress for me, a ceremonial scarf and a butter offering. In the meantime the *janggu* maintained a constant flow of ritual dialogue. The groom then gave the dress to the old man and tried to enter the house on horseback. After several such tries, everyone appealed to him to stop, and he finally got off his mount.

A sack of firewood, *tsampa*, three containers of barley and a mug decorated with motifs of the sun and moon were placed at the door. The girls waiting at the entrance and the astrologer were reciting prayers. My party dismounted and entered the house through the kitchen, where we washed our faces. I could not see, so my two female escorts led me by the hand to a huge pot of tea, made with milk, tea leaves and salt. Four cups were laid out in the four directions. I now had to stir the tea in three gestures. I filled and emptied a wooden tea jug three times, after which I filled the four cups to the brim. This was the opening ceremony.

The bridal party was then led into the main house, where we were asked to sit down. Men and women, old folks and children filled the rooms, and the singing began. The bridal party and the residents sang to each other in question-and-answer form, such as, 'We have come from afar and are drinking tea. What is the taste of water?'

In the evening a dinner was held. Once again songs played a pivotal role. My party sang to the cook in the kitchen, 'You are not nice, the food is tasteless, the radishes and the meat are raw.' The rejoinder from the groom's female household was, 'Don't you feel ashamed of yourselves, your stomachs are so big. You are a human being if you drink one cup of tea. But if you drink two or three cups of tea you are a cow.' The songs were a form of satire, scolding one another.

After this my trousseau was taken out of the trunk so a general inspection could take place, to display my mother's competence in embroidery and sewing. My possessions were then handed over to my in-laws, and everyone left the groom's house. No one was permitted to remain, not even me. I spent the night with my two women escorts at a neighbour's house. There the main meal was sweet rice with milk. I still had not met my husband-to-be.

The next day at about ten in the morning I was taken back to the groom's house, where another ceremony was performed. It was now time for me to formally don my *hari*, which I did outside the house. Though I had worn a *hari* to the groom's house, I was not permitted to fasten it properly, but had to wear it loose on both sides. After I was married it was secured firmly around my waist. The *hari* consisted of three main pieces, two at the sides and one down the back. The groom's family sent me the two side flaps, and my mother provided the central flap. The flaps had wool attached to them to hold them together. This wool was now cut with a pair of scissors. The person who cut the wool had to have a horoscope that accorded with mine. This person was presented with a ceremonial scarf and a cup of wine, and was formally requested to snip the *hari* with the scissors. This ceremony symbolised that I was now a married woman. I was now given my new name, Diki Tsering, by my mother-in-law's brother, Taktser Rinpoche.

It was customary for the groom to remain hidden and locked up somewhere during this stage of the proceedings. People would go and call for him but would not be able to find him. I was kept waiting while everyone searched for him. When they finally found him, they begged him to come from his hiding place, pleading that I was very tired, since I had come from so far away. My husband finally came forth and was presented with a ceremonial scarf. Only when my husband came out of his room was my *hari* finally secured. Only now did we set eyes on each other.

The next day my entire family and I returned to our home. Before leaving, my husband's family gave my party various parts of a sheep as presents, as well as festive bread. I met my mother-in-law for the first time on this day. She tenderly inspected me and spoke a few affectionate words, trying to comfort me. She gave me gifts of jewellery. I was to stay at my parents' home for a period from ten days to a month, according to the horoscope, after which my father would bring me back to my husband's house.

When I returned to my husband's house, a man and a woman received me at the door, together with an untainted person – widows, widowers, pregnant or barren women were not permitted to receive a bride – and a fertility rite was performed. I was presented with a bowl of milk, which I turned clockwise three times, after which I entered the house. I then poured *chang* for the male members of the household – my father-in-law and my husband's elder brother; my husband's grandparents had died long before. I was then taken to my room, escorted by all my husband's women kin.

I was not given any work for the first few days of my married life. I began household work only after five days. I did not even share a room with my husband at first, but stayed with the women folk. We began sharing a room after about three weeks. My husband was seventeen at the time of our marriage.

Once a daughter was married and given her share of the family property, she was no longer the responsibility of the natal home, but now owed allegiance to her in-laws and husband. Most families, for practical reasons, were reluctant to part with their daughter-in-law even for short periods of time. Though a daughter could return to her parent's home for visits lasting two to three months, her husband's family had to find a temporary replacement for her – generally a servant – to do her work until her return.

This happened with me, as my husband's family was small, and we had no extra help.

Daughters-in-law almost always had a very difficult life and were treated like servants or chattel. Some mothers-in-law drove their daughters-in-law like slaves, neither feeding nor clothing them properly, as a result of which many women, driven by desperation, committed suicide. Except for wives of officials, all women were expected to do hard labour and to work in cooperation with the servants. If the husband was dissatisfied with the marriage, he could end it at will. But no matter how ill-treated the daughter-in-law was, she could not utter a word of complaint, nor could she leave. It was her fate. If the daughter-in-law was very badly treated, her own family was permitted to take the case to court, but in those days laws generally favoured the in-laws. The position of the daughter-in-law improved after a few years of marriage, when she had attained a little more authority.

If a woman proved barren, her husband could contract a second marriage. A small marriage ceremony would take place, not as lavish as the first one. If the second wife also proved to be barren after a few years of marriage, then another wife would be taken, and so on until one of the wives bore children. Even if a husband had many wives, they all would remain in the same household. The first wife had the most power and highest status, despite the fact that she was barren. It was compulsory for the other wives to show her great respect. Adoption was quite frequent, provided there were no natural children and the husband did not want to remarry.

If a husband died, even when the wife was still young, she was not permitted to remarry until the three-year mourning period was over. It was a cruel custom, but a widow was always compelled to remarry, regardless of her wishes. She was never allowed to remain a widow. Her relatives would contract secret negotiations with interested parties and pay money in order that a man would marry her. The widow was bartered with no regard for her feelings, because she was considered a liability. I remember one unfortunate woman who was gagged and bound and removed forcibly in order that she remarry. Many widows jumped from cliffs and hanged themselves because of this custom.

Divorce did exist in Amdo at that time. A formal and mutual agreement was drawn up, in which the husband was the main signatory. He had to say that he was henceforth separating from his wife, and that she was free to remarry and lead her own life. If such a signed agreement did not exist, the divorce could not take place. Adultery was not tolerated in our area, as it was in other parts of Tibet. If any such instances took place, the woman would be killed by her own family. Such was the penalty.

11

Wifely Duties

After I was married I went to live in Taktser, about 25 km from Churkha. This area was famous for producing many female children and very few boys. For this reason the former Taktser Rinpoche built a *chorten*, or *stupa*[1], to assist women in giving birth to boys. It was said that after he built this *stupa*, more boys were born. Prior to this, girls never left their homes in marriage, but men were brought into the family to join the labour force.

Taktser was up on a rocky, steep hill, full of forests, so agriculture was difficult. There was no irrigation; for water we depended entirely upon the rains. My new house was one-storey. We lived in the inner courtyard, where we also had our flagpole for prayer flags. Animals were not permitted to come into this area. There was also an outer courtyard, where we had the stables and quarters for the servants.

[1] A *stupa* is a monument containing relics of the Buddha or other lamas, symbolising the mind of the Buddha.

My new home was about a nine-hour horse ride from my parents' home. I would see them about once a year, when my father would come and get me. Most women in our area would visit their parents after the sowing period, in the fourth month, when there was less work to be done. When I went home, my mother would make all my clothes for the whole year. In Tsongkha it was customary for the young women to be fashionable and to wear the newest and brightest of clothes. My mother would also make clothes for my in-laws and my husband, as gifts to ease the relationship between the families which, invariably, was strained.

At the outset of my marriage, most of the housework was done by my husband's sister. This sister had brought her husband into her family, but he was reluctant to stay with them, so they left for his family's home one month after my marriage. Thus I was left to do all the housework.

My mother-in-law had not married out; her husband had been brought into her family. She was not able to bear children for many years after her marriage, so in desperation she would go on pilgrimages, offering prayers for the birth of a son. She prayed to the goddess of fertility that if her wish was granted, she would supply the goddess with a set of clothing. On one occasion she went to a cave, where she was supposed to walk along in the dark until she could reach or touch some object. It was said that if your hand came across a snake, you would never conceive. Her hand came across a baby's shoe. Nine months later she conceived a son. After the birth of the child, she personally made a shoe, the mate to the one she had found, and made an elaborate set of clothing for the goddess and sent it to the monastery. She was 49 years old when she had her first son.

My mother-in-law never did a stroke of work. She was bossy and domineering, and was not afraid of anyone. She was led by her emotions and fancies, and liked to eat, dress and live well. She was extremely clean; if there was even one strand of grass in the house, she would pick it up and throw it away. She was also hot-tempered and was sometimes physically violent. I, being the daughter-in-law, had to take it all. Her sharp tongue made me the brunt of many miseries. If she was having her meal on the *kang*, I could not remain in the same room, but had to eat in the kitchen. Even then I had to always eat standing up.

Yet she was also warm-hearted and generous, and she shared everything fairly and equally. At times I was touched by her consideration. Because I worked in the fields, the ends of my sleeves would invariably get torn. My mother-in-law would attempt to stitch them for me, even though she could not sew well at all. I would always have to redo them, because she often made them worse than before.

My father-in-law was quite active on the farm, and would make two trips to the fields with the farm hands each day. He was a good and kind man. When I cut wheat and rolled it into sheaves, I could never tie them up, so he would assist me. He did not know how to scold a person. The most he ever said was, 'How incompetent', muttered under his breath. Whenever I broke any crockery, I dared not tell my mother-in-law, and I would bury the broken pieces. I would go to my father-in-law and tell him my tale of woe, weeping copiously. I still remember his words: 'Why didn't you hold the cup properly? If your mother-in-law asks you about this cup, tell her you didn't know about it. I'll say that I broke it instead.'

The husband-wife relationship in those days was not one of equality. The woman was always subservient to the man, even though she was supreme in domestic matters. My husband was an upright and honest man, straightforward, but powerful and domineering, with a hot temper. He was fond of gambling and having a good time, and loved riding swift horses. Like his mother, he did no work. He was never at home for very long and did not even know what we had sown in the fields.

One of my husband's brothers was the financial manager of the Kumbum monastery. He was a good person and treated me well. He told me that if my husband should ever beat me, I was to bring my daughter and come to stay with him at Kumbum. In fact, he used to scold my husband for not helping me at home, for always going off to have a good time. Both of my husband's sisters were very good to me too. Whenever they came to visit, they would always assist me in my work, even if it was only for a few minutes.

When my mother-in-law was alive, she was the

supreme authority, but after her death I took sole responsibility for looking after and supervising the servants, working in the fields, controlling the budget and buying and selling our agricultural produce.

I got up at one o'clock in the morning to fetch water for the servants and the farm hands. I went early in the morning because it was less crowded at that hour, but still we had to queue up. We had to bring the water up from the well very slowly in order not to disturb the sediment at the bottom. If we stirred the mud, the other women would fuss and provoke a fight. Sometimes I had to go to the well ten times in one day, but generally five or six times were enough. In winter my hands would freeze, so I would rub sheep's fat on them.

My in-laws would get up at about seven in the morning. I then had to make them tea, and my mother-in-law would scold me if I didn't get it fast enough. I had to sweep the floors of the house, light the stove and brew salted tea for the servants. The servants insisted upon salted tea, as they believed it would prevent stomach troubles. We would all have breakfast at about half past eight, and then the workers would leave for the fields. After this I would feed and milk the animals. Once every five or six days I had to clean out the *kangs* with a rake, and refill them with manure and straw.

I supplied the farm hands with their midday meal, carrying the food on my back to the fields. After giving them their lunch at about noon, I would join in the work. As we worked, we would ask those who could sing well to sing for us. We were very fond of singing. As the sun set at about five or six in the evening, the workers would sing as they slowly returned home.

But after work I would rush home frantically, for fear of receiving a scolding from my mother-in-law. I had to hurry to make dinner for the family and the servants. My mother-in-law would not even light the fire. If I did not prepare the dinner fast enough, she would beat me. After the death of my mother-in-law I did not work in the fields very much, as I had to look after my home and the children.

For the first few years after my marriage, I often had to make do with three or four hours of sleep at night. When we went to the mill to grind flour, it took eight to ten days, during which we did not sleep at all. We would thresh the flour from one o'clock in the morning to just before sunrise, then begin our day's work. I often felt unbearably tired. Sometimes, when I would go to collect manure for the *kang*, I would sit by the roadside and steal a few moments of sleep. Occasionally, under severe strain, I would go to a quiet place and shed a few pitiful tears, but I had my pride and would never weep in public. During those years of hardship I never told anyone that I was suffering, not even my husband.

12

Death and Mourning

*S*oon after I was married, my father-in-law died at the age of 63. I think that it must have been cancer, although in those days we did not even know the disease existed. He was not able to eat anything, or even retain honey, for a month. He had become terribly emaciated and weak, and we knew death was close. We had already hired the corpse-bearers.

On the night that he died, my father-in-law told me that although I had suffered a great deal from the sharp temper of my mother-in-law, my ordeal would hold me in good stead during the later years of my life. He told me not to take it to heart, and to be a good wife. I was weeping all the while. He tried to comfort me as best he could, telling me not to worry about him. Then he asked for a cup of tea and honey. As I lifted his head to give him a sip, he stopped breathing.

Everyone was called into the room and wept at his bedside. It was considered bad form to weep too much or to show an excess of emotion. So, trying to control ourselves, we prayed. All the neighbours came to the house to pay their last respects and to offer condolences and assistance to the family. After a death, twelve loaves of bread were presented to the family by visitors; twelve was the number of death. All the women in the house stopped work until the period of mourning was over, which was three weeks at that time. All the work was done by servants and hired hands.

All the family members would gather in the house during the three weeks of mourning, doing nothing but praying. Monks would come and say prayers for three days. These prayers were said so the soul of the deceased would have a beneficial transmigration, and to prevent his spirit from remaining in the house.

The astrologer determined how long the body was kept in the house; it could be up to three days. My father-in-law was kept in the house for two days. We kept watch over the body day and night, saying our rosaries and prostrating ourselves as many times as we could. We believe that at death the deceased becomes like a god, and so we treat him like one.

Astrologers also determined the best method for disposal of the corpse – by fire, by burial in the earth, by casting into the water or by being fed to the birds. Feeding to the birds was supposed to be the best method, as it was the cleanest, but in Tsongkha most bodies were buried. The corpse was arranged with legs crossed in the lotus position and the hands folded as in prayer.

Measurements were taken, and a wooden box was made to encase the body. The face was covered with a ceremonial scarf. The body was wrapped in white cloth, often some kind of silk. My father-in-law was wrapped in a white silk Tibetan dress. Sweet-smelling flowers and pine branches were laid with the body. Nothing else was put in the coffin.

Each family had their own burial ground within the confines of their compound, and it was to this place that my father-in-law was taken. All the neighbours came and said their last farewells. The astrologer also said which people could touch the dead body and the coffin. Male relatives had to shoulder the coffin, and they were not permitted to place it on the ground or even to stop, as it was believed that the deceased's soul would then remain in that spot and not take an appropriate rebirth.

The women relatives were not allowed to accompany the bier, but had to remain at home. My mother-in-law was very sad, and wept continuously. All her children came home to comfort her. For three weeks we could not visit anyone, and we could not ride horses. All the deceased's belongings were given away; nothing could be retained by his family.

Women were not permitted to decorate their hair with the normal colourful ribbons; nor were they permitted to wash their hair until a week after a death. Instead, our hair was roughly tied with a piece of white wool. Only old clothes could be worn, and all jewellery had to be removed. At the death of a father-in-law the brocade on the *hari* had to be removed from the left shoulder; at the death of a mother-in-law, from the right shoulder; at the death of one's parents, from the central piece down the back. It was worn this way as long as the mourning period lasted. When a husband died, brocade from both side flaps had to be removed for a period of three years.

Men in mourning were not permitted to wear new clothes, and if it was a parent who had died, they were not permitted to wear their customary hats. Like the women, they had to wear white woollen threads on their braids. After three weeks, these threads were discarded by both men and women and burned, and colourful ribbons could now adorn the hair.

Two years after my father-in-law died, my mother-in-law died. I was twenty; she was 58. She was sick, but I think she died from heartbreak at the death of her brother, Taktser Rinpoche, who had recently passed away.

When children died, the rites were simple. Lamas came to say prayers, and the astrologer made his calculations. I had three sons who died. One was buried, and the other two were taken to a high hill and left there for the birds of prey and the wild animals. I used to tell the corpse-bearers to bring back my children's clothes – they came into this world without clothes and I wanted them to leave it the same way.

We believed that if one wept too much when someone died, the dead would not find their final destination. It was said that parents' tears would be like hail on a dead child's face. So I always controlled myself when my children died, no matter how intense my suffering, and I would tell my husband not to cry, for the same reason.

13

Giving Birth

I had my first child, a daughter, at the age of nineteen. With each of my children I had a very easy labour because, as a peasant woman, I led an active life. Throughout each pregnancy I had to work as usual, even on the day of the birth. I ate special foods so that I would not get sick, and I never had morning sickness.

All women in those days were their own midwives. There was no such thing as going to the hospital or even having someone assist in child birth. Only with my first child did a maidservant assist me, and that was after the birth. She heard the whimpers of the child and came to cut and tie the umbilical cord. With all my other children I did everything myself. I had all my children in the stables, not in the house.

There was a great deal of reticence about the subject of childbirth in those days. Women never told anyone they were going to give birth. People knew that a child had been born only by its crying. There was no special birth ceremony as such, but neighbours would come and offer congratulations, making little gifts of baby clothes and blankets and bread. They would also give me sweet steamed rice with dates. One month after each birth, my family would hold a dinner in honour of the child. My daughter was given her name, Tsering Dolma, by a lama who used to say prayers in our house. Every month we would invite lamas to say prayers.

My mother-in-law gave me one week's rest after the birth of my first child. After the births of my other children, she was dead, and there was no one in the house to do the work, so I could rest for only a day or two. I'd take my babies to work on my back.

My mother-in-law was furious that I had given birth to a girl and not a boy, and her wrath fell on my husband. He tried to comfort her by saying that it was fate, that one could not will the sex of a child, but she was still very disappointed. Her brother, Taktser Rinpoche, had passed away, and she had hoped for a grandson so that he might be his new incarnation.

14

A Tulku Arrives

fter the death of Taktser Rinpoche, representatives from the monastery of Kumbum went to call on His Holiness the thirteenth Dalai Lama, in order to find the next incarnation, or *tulku*, of the abbot of Kumbum. When they arrived in Lhasa, they asked His Holiness to do a *thudam*, but His Holiness advised them that there was no incarnation as yet, and to come again the following year.

The following year the party returned to Lhasa. My brother-in-law, Ngawang Changchup, went along, as the financial manager of Kumbum. His Holiness told them that the incarnation had been born, and that it was within the vicinity of Kumbum, towards the east, where they have black dogs and horses. One of my neighbours had given birth to a boy, and it was this boy that was the new reincarnation. But His Holiness warned the party not to make proclamations or to finalise anything, but to return to Lhasa the following year.

My brother-in-law wept at this news, because they had already made the journey twice, and now they would have to return once more. He told His Holiness that the trip was very difficult for them, as they had to come so far. But His Holiness insisted that the time was not ripe for the new incarnation to be installed. He told them to stop weeping, that they could send a representative instead of having to travel such a distance themselves. He said they would be rewarded by a worthy lama. My brother-in-law thought it strange that His Holiness would not make a final decision, despite the fact that the new incarnation had been born.

Before their departure from Lhasa, the party went around to places of worship, taking with them butter offerings. At one of these places my brother-in-law noticed that the front of his brocade robe had been ruined with melted butter. No one had spilled the butter, so it was puzzling how it came to be on his robe. But he forbade the servants to remove the stains, saying this was a very good omen.

As he was nearing Tsongkha, monks from Kumbum came to receive him, and he asked them about the new incarnation. They told him that the child had died. Now he began to see the wisdom of His Holiness. He then enquired whether my child had been born, and was overjoyed to learn that I had given birth to a boy. He was now certain that my son would be the future incarnation of Taktser Rinpoche. I was 21 when I gave birth to Norbu, in the year of the Dog. A lama from Kumbum named him Tashi Tsering, but later he was given the monk's name Thubten Norbu.

The following year representatives from Kumbum went to Lhasa to see His Holiness once again. His Holiness gave the envoys a sealed letter, and delegated them to deliver the message to me that my son Tashi Tsering had been selected to be the next Taktser Rinpoche. There had been sixteen candidates for the position, all born in the year of the Dog. These children came from families that I was acquainted with; some were relatives, others were friends. All the families of the candidates were invited to our house for the formal verdict. The letter was then opened and the results were announced.

Both my husband and I were overjoyed. We thought immediately of my mother-in-law, who had so ardently wished that a son of ours be reborn as the Taktser Rinpoche. Now her wishes had been fulfilled. Even though we were the parents, we placed our son on a throne and presented him with ceremonial scarves. We had already decided to send him into the monastery, but now, instead of becoming an ordinary monk, he was elevated to the rank of a Rinpoche. Fate was indeed kind to us, and we wept many tears of joy. He was one year old at the time.

I was in Tsongkha expecting my son Lobsang Samten when my father died. I was later told that he was poisoned by some of his enemies while on a picnic. I could not go back home for the funeral, as I was far with child, and there was a possibility that I might give birth while on the road. Five days after my father's death, my son was born.[1]

[1] Diki Tsering gave birth to four children before the Dalai Lama was born in 1935: Tsering Dolma in 1919, Thubten Jigme Norbu in 1922, Gyalo Thondup in 1928 and Lobsang Samten in 1933. Two more children were to come: Jetsun Pema in 1940 and Tendzin Choegyal in 1946. These were the 7 children, of the 16 born to her, who survived past infancy.

15

Ocean of Wisdom

Almost three years after the birth of Lobsang Samten, I gave birth to Lhamo Dhondup, who would become the fourteenth Dalai Lama. My husband was bedridden with illness for two months prior to Lhamo Dhondup's birth. If he tried to stand up, he would feel giddy and lose consciousness. He told me that each time this happened, he would see the faces of his parents. He could not sleep at night, which was very difficult, because he kept me awake and I had to work during the day. I thought he was playing a cruel trick on me, but now I know this was not so. It was just one of a series of strange happenings in the three years that preceded the birth.

During that time our horses seemed to go mad, one by one. When we brought them water they would race for it and then begin rolling about in it. They could neither eat nor drink. Their necks stiffened and finally they could not even walk. All thirteen of them died. It was such a disgrace to the family and a great loss, as horses were money. After this there was a famine for three years. We had not a drop of rain, only hail, which destroyed all the crops. Everyone was at the point of starvation. Families began to migrate, until only 13 households were left out of 45. My family survived solely because the monastery of Kumbum supported us and supplied us with food. We lived on lentils, rice and peas that came from their stores.

Lhamo Dhondup was born early in the morning, before sunrise. To my surprise, my husband had got out of bed and seemed as if he had never been sick. I told him that I had had a boy, and he replied that this surely was no ordinary boy, and that we would make him a monk. Chushi Rinpoche from Kumbum had passed away and we hoped that this newborn infant would be his reincarnation. We had no more deaths or other strange incidents or misfortunes after his birth. The rains came, and prosperity returned, after years of destitution.

Lhamo Dhondup was different from my other children right from the start. He was a sombre child who liked to stay indoors by himself. He was always packing his clothes and his little belongings. When I would ask what he was doing, he would reply that he was packing to go to Lhasa, and that he would take all of us with him. When we went to visit friends or relatives, he would never drink tea from any cup but mine. He would never let anyone touch his blankets except me, and would never place them anywhere but next to mine. If he came across a quarrelsome person, he would pick up a stick and try to beat him. If ever one of our guests lit up a cigarette, he would flare into a rage. Our friends told us that for some unaccountable reason they were afraid of him, tender in years as he was. This was all when he was around a year old, and could hardly talk.

One day he told us that he had come from heaven. I had a strange foreboding then, for a month before his birth I had had a dream in which two green snow lions and a brilliant blue dragon appeared, flying about in the air. They smiled at me and greeted me in the traditional Tibetan style – two hands raised to the forehead. Later I was told that the dragon was His Holiness and the two snow lions were the Nechung oracle (the state oracle of Tibet), showing His Holiness the path to rebirth. After my dream I knew that my child would be some high lama, but never in my wildest dreams did I think that he would be the Dalai Lama.

When Lhamo Dhondup was a little more than two years old, the search party for the fourteenth Dalai Lama visited our home in Taktser. The party included Lobsang Tsewang, a *tsedun* (government official), Khetsang Rinpoche from Sera monastery (who was later tortured and killed by the Chinese), and others.

The first time they visited us was in the eleventh or twelfth month, and it was snowing heavily. There was about four feet of snow on the ground, and we were in the process of clearing it when they arrived. We did not recognise any of them, and realised that they must be from

Lhasa, although they did not tell us their mission.

They could speak the Tsongkha dialect fluently, as they had been in Tsongkha for three years searching for the Dalai Lama. They had been told that they would find His Holiness in the early morning, in a place that was all white. The party stopped at our door and said that they were on their way to Sanho, but had mistaken the road. They asked me to let them have some rooms for the night. I gave them tea, some of my homemade bread and dried meat.

Early the next morning they insisted on paying me for my hospitality and for the food for their animals. They said goodbye very warmly. After they left, we knew that this was the search party for His Holiness, but it never entered our minds that there was a purpose in their visit to our home.

Three weeks later the party returned to our home. This time they said they were going to Tsongkha, and could we please show them the road. My husband guided them to it himself, and they left.

After two weeks they came back a third time. This time Khetsang Rinpoche was carrying two staffs as he entered our veranda, where Lhamo Dhondup was playing. Rinpoche put both staffs in a corner. Our son went to the staffs, laid one aside and picked up the other. He struck Rinpoche lightly on the back with it, said the staff was his and why had Khetsang Rinpoche taken it. The party members exchanged mean-

Right The Dalai Lama as a very young child.

Below The Potala Palace in Lhasa, the ceremonial home of His Holiness. 'It was a museum, the grandeur of which I will never see again.'

Left Diki Tsering, known as Gyayum Chenmo, 'Great Mother', in traditional dress in front of the Potala Palace.

Above A pair of *dzo*, the cross between a bull and a yak. These are farm animals typically used for plowing fields. '[Our] stables were separate, and there we kept our sheep, cows, horses and *dzomo*. A *dzomo* is the offspring of a yak and a cow. The male is called a *dzo*.'

Below Tents of high Tibetan government officials.

Above The Chinese People's Liberation Army marches into Lhasa carrying portraits of Chairman Mao and Marshal Chu Teh.

Below A group of Tibetan resistance fighters.

Above His Holiness and the Panchen Lama are welcomed to the Peking railway station by Premier Chou En-lai and Marshal Chu Teh. 'I was afraid for [our] safety for the Chinese were not what they seemed.'

Right His Holiness at age nineteen addresses the National People's Congress in Peking. His Holiness thought that his attempts at peaceful coexistence would persuade the Chinese to adhere to the Seventeen-Point Agreement.

Above Members of the Chinese Communist Government sign the Seventeen-Point Agreement in Peking.

Below Diki Tsering and Mrs Taring in China, with the wife of a Chinese official and her daughter. Mrs Taring later accompanied Diki Tsering on a visit to England.

Above His Holiness travels in the centre palanquin in this formal procession from the Potala Palace to Norbulingka monastery.

Below Tucked into a mountain valley is the Drepung monastery. Founded in AD 1416, this is the largest monastery in the world. Before 1959 it housed 7,000 monks.

Above Diki Tsering, His Holiness, and their entourage escape on horseback from Communist-controlled Tibet. 'We rode non-stop and at great speed. When we stopped, I could barely stand, from a mixture of cold, fatigue and cramps in my legs. It had been very windy and thick dust caked my face.'

Left His Holiness crosses the border to India. 'It was a relief to be safe. We had privacy and peace [in India]; [now] the Chinese were very far away and did not give me any cause for panic.'

Left Diki Tsering and His Holiness. '[He] was different from my other children right from the start.'

Right Diki Tsering, surrounded by her family, at their home in Dharamsala, India.

ingful looks, but I could not understand a word of the Lhasa dialect they spoke.

I was in the kitchen later, drinking tea on the *kang*, when Khetsang Rinpoche joined me there. It was easy to converse with him, as he could speak both Tsongkha and Chinese fluently. As we sat there, Lhamo Dhondup stuck his hand beneath Rinpoche's heavy fur robes and seemed to tug at one of the two brocade vests he was wearing. I scolded my son, telling him to stop pulling at our guest. He drew a rosary from under Rinpoche's vest and insisted it was his. Khetsang Rinpoche spoke gently to him, saying that he would give him a new one, that the one he was wearing was old. But Lhamo Dhondup was already removing his clothes in order to put on the vest. I later learned that this vest had been given to Khetsang Rinpoche by the thirteenth Dalai Lama.

That evening we were summoned by the party. They were seated on the *kang* in their room. In front of them was a bowl of candy, two rosaries and two *damarus* (ritual hand drums). They offered our son the candy bowl, from which he selected one piece and gave it to me. He then went and sat with them. From a very young age Lhamo Dhondup always sat eye-to-eye with everyone, never at their feet, and people told me that I was spoiling him. He then selected a rosary from the table and a *damaru*, both of which, it turned out, had belonged to the thirteenth Dalai Lama.

Our guests offered my husband and me a cup of tea and ceremonial scarves. They insisted that

I take some money as their way of thanking me
for my hospitality. When I refused, they told me
to keep it as a sign of auspiciousness. They said
they were looking for the fourteenth Dalai
Lama, whom they were certain had been born
somewhere in Tsongkha. There were sixteen
candidates, they said. In truth they had already
decided upon my son. Lhamo Dhondup spent
three hours with them that evening. They later
told me that they had spoken to him in the
Lhasa dialect, and that he had replied without
difficulty, although he had never heard that
dialect before.

Later Khetsang Rinpoche drew me aside and,
addressing me as 'mother', said that I might
have to leave my home and go to Lhasa. I
answered that I did not want to go – that I could
not leave my home with no one to look after it.
He replied that I should not say that, because I
would have to go when the time came. He said
not to worry about my home, that if I left I
would live very comfortably and not have any
difficulty. He was going to Tsongkha to see the
local governor, Ma Pu-fang, to tell him that the
Dalai Lama had been born in Tsongkha, and
that they were planning to take him to Lhasa.

Early the next morning, as they prepared to
leave, Lhamo Dhondup clung on to Khetsang
Rinpoche and wept, begging to go along.
Rinpoche comforted him, saying he would
come back to get him in a few days. Then he
bowed low and touched his forehead to my
son's.

After they met Ma Pu-fang, they returned

once more. This time they said there were three candidates for the Dalai Lama. These three boys had to go to Lhasa, and one would be chosen under the image of Je Rinpoche. Their names would be put in a bowl, they said, and with a pair of gold chopsticks the name would be selected. In fact they had already decided upon my son. I said again that I could not go, whereupon Khetsang Rinpoche spoke frankly to me, saying that I definitely had to leave for Lhasa. He confirmed that my son was the fourteenth Dalai Lama, but told me to keep it to myself.

Four days later, four envoys from Ma Pu-fang arrived at our home, took photographs of our house and family, and told us that we were to leave for Tsongkha the next day, on the orders of Ma Pu-fang. I was in the eighth month of my pregnancy, and said that I was unable to go. But they told me it was compulsory and important. They said that the families of all 16 candidates had been summoned.

It took eight hours on horseback to get to Tsongkha. I felt acute discomfort on the journey and had to rest every hour or so. Once in Tsongkha, we were put up in a hotel. My husband and his uncle took my son to Ma Pu-fang's residence. There all the children were told to sit in a semi-circle in chairs. The other children cried and refused to let go of their parents' hands, but my son, with great dignity for his young age, went directly to the only vacant seat and settled himself. When the children were offered candy, many of them grabbed handfuls, but my son took one piece, which he immedi-

ately gave to my husband's uncle. Ma Pu-fang
then asked Lhamo Dhondup whether he knew
who he was. Without hesitation he replied that
the man was Ma Pu-fang.

Ma Pu-fang said that if there was a Dalai
Lama, then it was this boy, the brother of
Taktser Rinpoche. He said that this boy was different, with his big eyes and his intelligent conversation and actions, that he was dignified far
beyond his years. He dismissed the other families and told my husband and me that we were
to remain in Tsongkha for a few days. For twenty days Ma Pu-fang looked after us and our
steeds. On the fourteenth day I gave birth to a
baby who died soon afterwards. Each day Ma Pu-
fang sent food for us and for the animals, as well
as money for daily expenses. He told us to
regard him as a friend. He said we were not ordinary people and were not his prisoners, but that
we would be going to Lhasa. We were so happy
at the news, but our tears were both of joy and
sorrow. I was sad to leave my native land and all
that I had known for 35 years. With a mixture of
apprehension and anticipation I left Tsongkha,
for an uncertain future.

I later heard that Ma Pu-fang demanded of
the Tibetan government an exorbitant ransom
in exchange for the departure of my son. The
government complied with his blackmail, only
to be met with another ransom demand for
more money. This money was borrowed from
Muslim traders, who were going on a pilgrimage
to Mecca via Lhasa, and who were to accompany
us on our journey there. I also heard that Ma Pu-

fang was not satisfied with this second ransom and demanded that a hostage of the government be left behind, to be released on news of the safe arrival of His Holiness. The search party therefore left behind Lobsang Tsewang. Later this man escaped from the custody of Ma Pu-fang and returned safely to Lhasa.

Khetsang Rinpoche informed me of all this. My husband and I told Rinpoche that they had made a serious error in telling Ma Pu-fang the truth. They should have told him that we were going on a pilgrimage, and then none of this unpleasantness would have arisen. Rinpoche acknowledged his mistake, but he said it was wiser to have spoken the truth in case they had been stopped on the journey.

I had known Ma Pu-fang since childhood, as he was acquainted with my father's two brothers. He had inherited the governorship from his father. China was in upheaval at this time. Civil war between the Kuomintang and the Communists was raging. When the Communists gained control of China, Tsongkha fell to that faction. I heard that Ma Pu-fang escaped to Arabia, where he took up a teaching post.

Finally Ma Pu-fang informed us that we were to leave for Kumbum, where preparations for our journey to Lhasa were being made. He gave us a gift of four swift steeds and a tent, and said that if we were in trouble we must inform him. I had just given birth, and social protocol outside traditional village life demanded that a woman not leave the house until a month after a birth. But my brother-in-law from Kumbum told me that this was a special case, and allowances would be made for me, so it would not be a breach of the moral code.

Six days after the birth of my child (the daughter who died soon after) we left for a stay of three weeks at Kumbum. There I spent my days making clothes for everyone for the journey. Others at the monastery were also busy making preparations.

My husband and I then returned to Taktser one final time, to settle affairs on the farm. Once I got there I had to prepare grass and fodder for our pack animals and horses. As most of the route to Lhasa was barren, uninhabited terrain, I had to make ample provisions for the animals. I also packed a lot of Tsongkha tea, *chang*, vinegar, dates, persimmons and new clothes for my family. Since the Kumbum monastery was like a home for us, we gave them custody of all important articles from our home. We invited them to say prayers for our forthcoming journey, and we invited all our neighbours and relatives for meals, to bid them goodbye. We were soon to leave forever.

Our relatives wept that they might never see us again. We Amdo folk are very emotional and sentimental, and sorrow, except to protect the loved ones at the time of death, is shown by tears. Our relatives journeyed with us for several days, and then they returned to their homes. I wept so much that I was blinded most of the day of our departure. We could not even bid each other farewell, so choked were our voices.

After this we returned to Kumbum. One day

two monks came to me and said they had heard some unfortunate news – that Lhamo Dhondup was not the real Dalai Lama, but that it was a boy from Lopon. They said this in order to tease my son. When they left, to my surprise, I found my son in tears, sighing miserably. When I asked him what the matter was, he said that what the two monks had said was untrue, that he was the real Dalai Lama. I tried to comfort him, saying that the monks had been playing a trick on him. After a great deal of assurances he felt better.

I asked him why he was so attracted to Lhasa, and he said that he would have good clothes to wear and would never have to wear torn clothes. He always disliked wearing tattered clothes, and he disliked dirt. If there was even a spot of dust on his shoes he would refuse to wear them. Sometimes he would deliberately aggravate a tear by tearing it further. I would admonish him, saying I did not have the money to make new clothes for him. He would reply that when he grew up he would give me a lot of money.

II.

Mother of Compassion

16

The Long Journey

We left for Lhasa on the third day of the sixth month in 1939. The date and time for our departure had been set by the astrologers in Lhasa. My mother had come to Kumbum to see us off, but as she was old she came no further. She begged me to return to Tsongkha after a year or two. If I had known that it would be many years before I was to see our home again, my sorrow at leaving would have been all the greater.[1]

Our contingent included me, my husband, Lhamo Dhondup, my sons Gyalo Thondup and Lobsang Samten, and my husband's elder brother, Ngawang Changchup, the senior steward of Kumbum. My eldest son, Taktser Rinpoche, stayed behind at the monastery, as did my daughter. We left them with the hope that if the situation in Lhasa was amenable, we would send for them.

---

[1] Some accounts have recorded the date of departure as 21 July 1939.

It was supposed to be a secret that my son had been selected as the fourteenth Dalai Lama, but word soon spread, and many villagers met our caravan, seeking an audience. But while we were still in Chinese territory, no audiences were permitted, because it was too dangerous. We told people that this child was only one of the candidates for the Dalai Lama. Two days out of Kumbum we arrived at Tulku monastery, outside Chinese territory. In the shrine room there a long-life offering ceremony was conducted, after which local people came for audiences.

Along the way, some Sangsang tribesmen came and greeted us. To me, coming from Tsongkha, they seemed very dirty and I criticised them for this. His Holiness became furious that I was judging people by their physical appearance. He was four years old.

From Tulku we went on to Tsaidam, where we spent ten days. Two to three hundred people came to see His Holiness every day. From here we went to Koko Nor, where we pitched our tents for three days. It was barren, dry terrain, with no mountains – not even any birds. At some places the grass was so bad that if the horses were to eat it they would become ill and die. In these places we would drape the horses' mouths with cloth to prevent them from grazing. We saw many wild animals on the journey – asses, mountain goats and bears. At night the wild asses would cause panic among the horses, which would scatter. What a headache this caused the horsemen, who had to recover the horses!

When wild asses were spotted, guns were immediately fired in the air to ward them off.

The journey from Kumbum to Lhasa lasted almost three months[2]. There were more than a thousand people in our retinue, and thousands of animals. It was no easy matter to travel day in and day out for months at a stretch. If we were travelling in territory renowned for banditry, or where it was too cold to spend the night, we would be on the move for 24 hours before we came to a halt.

Such a tiring journey was made more so by the great urgency of our arriving at Lhasa soon. We travelled as fast as we could. We would rise at three in the morning, and the tent-bearers would fold the tents and proceed ahead of us. The tents were enormous, as large as houses. We never had breakfast – if we had we would soon afterwards feel pangs of hunger. If we abstained, we didn't feel hungry until the next stop.

His Holiness was carried with Lobsang Samten in a palanquin drawn by horses. I had a separate palanquin drawn by four mules. The palanquins were embroidered, with little lattice windows, and were very pretty. His Holiness's palanquin was made of yellow brocade, while mine was of green cotton. Gyalo Thondup was eleven years of age at the time. No matter how much I insisted that he ride with me, he would instead go on horseback. He had inherited his love of horses from his father. Without telling

[2] The party arrived in Lhasa on 8 October 1939.

me, he would accompany the tent-bearers, leaving early in the morning.

We went by way of Namkatse, Piti, Tsaidam and Dugdug. There were no proper roads most of the way, only grasslands. When we came to the river at Dijughu, it took the animals half an hour to swim across. They were sent across as fast as they could go, or else they would have sunk into the soft sediment.

The first emissaries from Lhasa – aristocrats and officials – were waiting for us at Dugdug. Later we were met by Suthupa and Kungo Khenpo at Wamathang. Government officials came to Drichu and presented me with pearl and coral *patus*, the Lhasa women's headdresses, and brocade dresses and other accessories worn by the ladies of Lhasa. I refused to wear the *patu*. I said that I had worn my *hari* since I was sixteen and would not feel comfortable with the *patu*, which was too heavy.

When we arrived at Reting monastery, we were welcomed by Reting Rinpoche, the regent, a young man in his thirties who was overseeing the government in the interim between Dalai Lamas. (It was Reting who had seen a vision in a lake that led to the discovery of the fourteenth Dalai Lama.) He asked what I thought of the *patu*. When I told him I was going to keep on wearing my *hari*, he said it was very beautiful. He said that wearing one's traditional clothes was an excellent idea, and that His Holiness's mother should be different. He was greatly taken with my *hari*. When I told him that I had created the elaborate designs, he said that he would call on me in Lhasa and request me to embroider the Gelukpa monks' headgear.

To my surprise the regent Reting then began to describe the details of our house in Takster, which he had seen in a vision. He knew that there was a tree in the backyard and a *stupa* (a reliquary mound) at the doorway, and that we had a small black-and-white dog and a large mastiff on the terrace. He noted that there were many nationalities in our house and asked who they were. I said they were Muslims and Chinese, whom we had hired to work in the fields.

He remarked that the Amdo people were very straightforward and honest, with clear hearts, and although they were hot-tempered, their anger went away as quickly as it arose. He warned me that the people in Lhasa, on the other hand, had less transparent hearts. He said we would meet many different types of people in Lhasa, and some would be genuinely warm and sincere, but others would try to harm us. He warned me about the government officials, saying they were experienced flatterers. Superficially they would be gentle, but you might never know what they were feeling inside. He warned me to be careful of what I ate, and never to accept food that had not been cooked in my personal kitchen, as it might be poisoned.

We stayed three days at Reting monastery, where the monks held a big reception to welcome their new Dalai Lama. We were lavishly entertained, and were even shown *lhamo*, Tibetan opera. From Reting it was three days to

Lhasa. On the way we were met by numerous monk officials, lay officials and aristocrats, as well as the abbots of the three monasteries of Sera, Ganden and Drepung, who came seeking an audience with His Holiness. They presented him with the traditional ceremonial scarf, and to me they presented lavish silks and brocades.

After leaving Reting we stayed at Reja, a monastery on a hill, for two days as the astrological forecast was unfavourable for our arrival in Lhasa at the scheduled time.

Reting Rinpoche accompanied us, as well as the Kashag (the Dalai Lama's Council of Ministers), high-ranking monks and *khenpos* (scholar monks), in procession. The army flanked us on the left and right. It was an occasion of austerity, solemnity and joy. Ceremonial music accompanied us all the way. As soon as I saw the city of Lhasa from a distance, there was a lump in my throat. I had heard so much about this city and had so often dreamed of it, and I now saw my dreams coming true.

17

Arrival in Lhasa

At Reting I had left my palanquin and was now riding on horseback. His Holiness moved to a more elaborate, gilded palanquin, which was carried on the shoulders of eight bearers. The crowds that greeted us as we entered Lhasa were overwhelming. There were so many people that we could hardly make any progress. The crowds were completely silent, with palms together and heads bowed, out of respect and greeting to their new Dalai Lama. Many people were weeping tears of joy. I was close to tears. Here I was, a peasant woman, now raised to the highest position a mother could hold.

As soon as we arrived in Lhasa, we were taken to Norbulingka ('Jewel Park'), the summer residence of the Dalai Lama. His Holiness was escorted to his private chambers and a ceremony of welcome was conducted. All the assembled were given Tibetan tea and *domadesi* (a kind of pastry). Then my family and I were shown to our chambers, very near those of His Holiness's.

When we entered our rooms we found many sacks of rice, flour, butter and tea that had been sent as gifts. Silks, brocades and carpets were brought in, and we were presented with ceremonial scarves. The next day the government supplied us with staff members – secretaries, interpreters, servants, stablemen, a water bearer, kitchen workers, maidservants, cooks – along with abundant provisions.

I was surprised to see His Holiness breaking the seals of the many trunks he found in his quarters, searching for something. Finally he found what he was looking for – a small box covered in brocade. I asked him what he was doing, and he told me that inside this box was a tooth. When he opened it, indeed there was a tooth, which had belonged to the thirteenth Dalai Lama.

We had arrived in the eighth month, when all the fruits were ripening, and Norbulingka was filled with flowers. Never before had I remained idle, and now I was living in heaven, a lotus land. We would spend all day in the gardens, picking apples, pears and walnuts. My son Lobsang Samten resided in the chambers of His Holiness, as a sort of companion. They had lessons and meals and played together.

In the first week of our stay at Norbulingka we had many visitors – lay and monk officials, and aristocrats and their wives – who came to pay their respects. I often felt foolish at receiving so much attention, particularly as I had to communicate through an interpreter. Many people showed great interest in my life at Tsongkha and the journey to Lhasa. For three months we led a life of luxury.

After a while I began to find it frustrating to be waited on and not do any work. Though great honour had now become my fate, I wept inside for my home. There I had had to work hard to support my family, but I had been at peace and extremely happy. I had had freedom and privacy. Now I was treated like a queen, but I was not as happy as I had been in Tsongkha. I had found it satisfying to work hard and to witness the fruits of my labour. To succeed with my crops and with my home and family was to me the epitome of a good life.

18

A New Life Begins

ive months after our arrival in Lhasa, His Holiness moved to the Potala Palace. It is an imposing edifice, made more so by its location on a hill. At first I was overwhelmed. It would take me twenty minutes to walk up the stone steps to reach the top of the thirteen storeys. There seemed to be no end to the gold and silver decorations and elaborate wall *thangkas* (religious paintings on cloth scrolls) that filled the rooms. It was a museum, the grandeur of which I will never see again. I was particularly taken by the icons of the previous Dalai Lama, which were made of solid gold. When I first arrived at the Potala it seemed familiar, as if I had been there many times before. While in Tsongkha, before the birth of His Holiness, I had had numerous dreams of the Potala, and I was amazed to see that the rooms were exactly as I had seen in my dreams.

On all sides of the Potala were wooden entrance doors with huge iron locks. There were certain rules for entering the premises, listed on huge signs in the main entrance: no foreign hats or foreign shoes, no knives and no guns within the premises. Tibetan boots and hats were permitted.

We used to go to the Potala by horseback for all the ceremonies. During Losar (Tibetan New Year) since there were so many events, we were given chambers at the top of the Potala, complete with two kitchens and a room to meet people.

In the beginning I was not familiar with many of the customs of Lhasa, since they were so different from those in Tsongkha. I would cautiously watch what other people did, so that I would not make any mistakes. I could go out whenever I wanted, taking my maidservants with me. My life was restricted only by social protocol, and that was to be expected. I never visited the marketplace or the little shops, for instance; I would see them only from horseback. I did visit Sera, Drepung, Ganden – practically all the monasteries of note. The best were Sera and Drepung.

When His Holiness was eleven or twelve, he had his first examinations at Drepung. I spent ten days there with him. Since women were not permitted to stay in the main building of the monasteries, I stayed in a guest house in the courtyard with my family. A few thousand spectators would attend his exams. Similar examinations were conducted by the scholars of Sera and then Ganden. Being a mother, I would be so nervous that His Holiness would not do well when he was questioned by the leading scholars, but my fears were unfounded, as he always came up to expectations.

I was a novice in matters of diplomacy and had much to learn about Lhasa society. As a peasant, I was brought up in an atmosphere of honesty and sincerity, both of which were greatly stressed in Tsongkha. Intrigue was unknown to me, and I had yet to learn that the world could be cruel and hard. Gradually I came to learn that Lhasa society was not what I had been brought up to believe.

Madame Lalu, who belonged to a prominent Lhasa family, became a good friend of mine. She was one of the few people in Lhasa who gave me solid advice on circumspection and reticence when in the company of the aristocrats. At that time I could not speak the language, and I did not want my words misinterpreted. (It took me two years to learn the Lhasa dialect.) Mr Tsarong's mother also became a good friend, as did Madame Ragashar, both members of the nobility. All three voiced the same opinion, warning me not to be too frank or to voice too many opinions to the people who came to visit me. I was indeed grateful to these three wonderful friends for their kind advice. But their words caused me great alarm and apprehension, and I was afraid for the future.

Madame Ragashar would often come to visit, asking if I was busy. I would say I didn't have much to do, and she would propose a game. We would then bring out the Chinese checker board. We had some fine games of checkers. She would then tell me stories and perhaps gossip a little, as all women do when they get together.

After our arrival in Lhasa we were given some property that had belonged to the thirteenth Dalai Lama. He had been approached by the British Legation to sell the land but he refused, saying that it would be useful to him later on. It was called Changseshar, meaning 'Eastern Garden'. It was a huge property filled with trees. A lot of *thudam* was done by the Nechung oracle to find the most auspicious sites for the buildings. Our house was of stone and had three storeys and pillars. It was constructed by the government. A two-storey house was built beyond the courtyard. After three years at Norbulingka, we moved to this new home, escorted by the army in a grand procession of two hundred men and musicians. We resided there until 1959.

In Lhasa we had many servants. We had a *chang-zo*, who received letters and replied to them, a financial manager, and a secretary who assisted him. The *nyerpa* was in charge of the household stores and everything pertaining to them. I had two maidservants, my daughter had two servants and one maidservant to look after the children, my husband had six servants and my son Gyalo Thondup had four. We had two kitchens, one for the servants and one for the family members. In each there was a chef, a dishwasher and a vegetable cleaner. The head stableman tended our five hundred horses, assisted by many stableboys.

In Tsongkha we had our own land, which our family tilled with the assistance of servants. But in Lhasa the *miser* (bonded labourers) did all the work, while the masters lived off them. It angered me to see that some families treated their *miser* with contempt. Sometimes the *miser* travelled six or seven days from their land, merely to bring us produce, and my *chang-zo* and *nyerpa* would not even speak to them or acknowledge their presence. After a few scoldings from me, this treatment stopped among the members of my household. I insisted that they call the *miser* by their names, rather than *kei* and *mei* (man and woman).

I would get up at six in the morning, kowtowed two hundred times and then said prayers. Breakfast was at half past eight. I spent most of my days in the gardens of Changseshar, and only left the house when the occasion demanded – to visit His Holiness, to go to sacred places of worship, or to go to the Potala for important festivals. I went to sleep at nine at night.

After about a year in Lhasa, I sent my son Gyalo Thondup to Seshing school. He was there for two years, after which he left for China. He was very naughty at school, always playing truant, going with his friends to fly kites. One day his teacher caught him at this mischief and gave him a caning. I was furious because I thought it wrong that children should be beaten severely, but later I came to see that it was my son's fault. After this he did not play truant again.

The year after our arrival at Lhasa, my husband invited my daughter and son-in-law to stay with us. Some traders were returning to Tsongkha, and he instructed them to bring them back. Tsering Dolma was our only daughter at that time, and we wanted to have her with us. One year after her arrival, my son Norbu (Taktser Rinpoche) joined us, and so the entire family was reunited. Norbu remained with us for one year, studying his lessons, after which he left for Drepung monastery. Six years later he went back to Kumbum to receive the rank of abbot, and remained there three years. My son Lobsang Samten remained with His Holiness for more than two years, and then it was decided to send him to school at Seshing, where he remained for one year. After that he was also sent to Drepung monastery.

19

Strange Customs

There is a certain amount of snobbery in any society, and Lhasa was no exception. Many people in the higher ranks of that society regarded us with contempt because we were tillers of the soil. We were regarded as outsiders because we came from Amdo. I heard all this a few years after we arrived. Of course, it was never said directly by those who looked down on us, but close friends of mine told me.

I'm sure that most of the women thought it a little odd that I wore the *hari*, though they did not say so. Lhasa was a fashionable society, and I must have seemed a little outdated. The wives of aristocrats and lay officials were very fashion-conscious, and seemed to be trying to outdo one another in their finery. When I first arrived, I was amazed to see how magnificently they dressed, wearing the finest jewellery. But what astounded me the most was how much make-up they wore. I had never before seen women painting themselves with rouge, lipstick or face powder. I thought these perfectly made-up women were actresses in the opera, and I was greatly surprised to learn that they were ordinary women. They looked like dolls. I thought all this was rather superficial.

Madame Lalu used to make herself up rather heavily, and she tried to persuade me to adorn my face a little. I never could, for I would feel self-conscious and uncomfortable. Even my husband and Gyalo Thondup were influenced by the local fashion: they had their right ears pierced for turquoise earrings.

I was also astonished at other customs. I saw women, one month before the birth of their child, sitting in the sun naked, with well-greased stomachs. I was told that it was so they would have an easy birth. I also saw mothers place their newly born infants in the sun, completely naked and slathered with oil.

A few years after I arrived in Lhasa, women began to see doctors when they were pregnant. The doctors were mostly Chinese, and they would instruct women to have their babies delivered at the Chinese hospital. But women were often reluctant to go, due to a certain reticence about their bodies. Tibetan medical institutions never delivered babies. The leading aristocratic women would deliver their babies at Indian hospitals. It was common for these women to breastfeed their babies for three days, after which the children would be taken by maid servants.

When a baby was only three days old, women in Lhasa would melt butter, mix in some *tsampa*, and feed it to the child. In Tsongkha we would supplement the mother's milk with the milk of the *dzomo*, but we did not give children solid food until around five months. At that time we would grind broad beans into a fine powder, roast it and mix it with milk and molasses. We also gave babies dried dates that had been soaked in hot water.

In Tsongkha women were not permitted to attend rituals immediately after childbirth, as they were considered polluted. But in Lhasa women took their newborn infants to temples and monasteries three days after their birth.

In Lhasa aristocratic daughters did not have to do much work, except perhaps a little embroidery; domestic chores were not emphasised. Girls were sent to school to be educated. Marriage customs, however, were very similar to those in Amdo.

20

Losar in Lhasa

*P*reparations for New Year at the Potala started three months prior to Losar, with the making of *kabse* (fried bread). For each ceremony an entire roomfull of *kabse* was used. The day before Losar we cleaned the house, changed the curtains, decorated the altars and piled up the *kabse* beside the altar. In the evening we had a dinner for friends and relatives.

On Losar we would rise at one in the morning, make offerings to His Holiness at our family altar and take our seats in the drawing room. Staff members would then offer us Losar greetings, along with Tibetan tea and *domadesi. Kodan* – brewed sweet *chang* – along with cheese and *tsampa* was served. Scarves were presented to us by the staff, in order of rank. After this we would leave immediately for the Potala, to participate in the early-morning ceremony that began at two o'clock.

The ceremony opened with prostrations to His Holiness by all those gathered, in order of rank – government staff, members of the British Legation and Muslim and Chinese representatives. Everyone would present His Holiness with a scarf, and he would give blessings, all of which could take two to three hours. During the ceremony we would be served all sorts of delicacies at regular intervals – Tibetan tea, *tsampa* with meat, *domadesi* with yogurt. The *tsampa* was soft and delicious, and the tea was made from fresh leaves and the best butter.

After the drummers and dancers performed, it was customary for the participants to grab the *kabse* offerings and take as much as they could. It was amusing to watch, as there was such a rush for all the delicacies. It was also customary to make a show of violence, and for the guards to strike at the crowds rushing for the food. It is said that the origin of this custom began with the twelfth Dalai Lama, who saw it in a dream.

We then returned home, because this first day of Losar was when we had to receive callers – aristocratic families and government officials. On this day at home we would generally serve Mongolian hotpot.

On the second day of Losar, we all attended a ceremony at the Potala at eight in the morning. There were more formalities than on the first day. Again the prostrations and blessings came first, a protocol that occurred at all large and important ceremonies. *Domadesi* and Tibetan tea were served, as well as other delicacies such as fried bread filled with meat. On this day the state oracles made predictions for the coming year. We again received callers, as on the first day, and members of the family took New Year offerings to the Kashag (the Cabinet) and government officials as well as to the lamas.

On the fourth day of New Year began Monlam – the Great Prayer Festival. Strict rules had to be observed by everyone during Monlam: no noise, including no barking dogs and no singing, and no intoxicating spirits. The night before, monks came from other monasteries to Lhasa, where they were housed with local families. Early the next morning the lamas proceeded to the Jokhang, and soon all three of its floors were teeming with monks, like ants on a hill.

If His Holiness was visiting the Monlam ceremonies, my family and I would go for a few hours to a special seating area in the Jokhang, invisible from public view, where we could watch the events from the windows. We would generally go on the eighth and fifteenth of the month, days considered auspicious. Except for these two days, we did not leave the house for the twenty days of Monlam. We could see all the activities from the terraces of Changseshar.

What I found amusing during the Monlam festival were the tea bearers. They wore quite a distinctive uniform – a Tibetan dress falling to just below the knees, no trousers and no socks. They looked a sight carrying huge copper or brass vessels on their shoulders, running around in bare feet serving tea.

Sometimes I would go and watch the cooks making food for the Monlam participants. I used to laugh at them trying to stir the huge pots. They would have to stand up on tables in order to reach them, and it would take a few people to stir one pot. If they were making rice porridge, a hundred sacks of rice and thirty whole sheep would be cooked for one meal.

Towards the end of Monlam there were archery and horse-racing competitions. Each family would supply a certain number of competitors and horses. Each competitor had to wear a suit of armour and an iron helmet. This was an ancient military custom.

Although we participated in the Lhasa Losar festival, at home we still celebrated the Amdo Losar as well. In fact, we celebrated all the Amdo festivals throughout the year. Our employees were surprised when special food was cooked for them, and we would tell them that it was an Amdo festival.

21

Grandmother and Widow

In 1940, two years after our arrival in Lhasa, while we were still at Norbulingka, I gave birth to a daughter, Jetsun Pema. Her name was given to her by His Holiness. I later had two sons, one of whom died at two years of age, in 1945. Both these sons were born at Changseshar. The son who lived was named Tenzing Choegyal; he was born in 1946. The son who died was called Tenzing Chota. He was so lively. He would go to His Holiness's chambers and upset everything. He died after a bronchial infection that lasted many months. When he died we invited the Gadong oracle to do a *thudam*.

Both the Gadong and Nechung oracles would go into a trance together in the personal chambers of His Holiness in times of crisis. After an oracle died, another was immediately installed. At the time of his selection, he was taken before His Holiness, who tested his powers by throwing some grain at him. If his power was not strong, this would make his powers wilt, but if he was a powerful medium, he was strengthened by this action. The Nechung was the state oracle for His Holiness and for the government. He was a monk and was not permitted to go to people's homes. The Gadong could go to certain homes, like ours. He was a layman, with a wife and children. He had his own monastery close to Drepung. I had many contacts with the Nechung and Gadong oracles.

It was routine that on the day before the oracle was to go into a trance, he had to maintain certain purificatory rites. He abstained from flesh and onions, and spent the day cleansing his system, because the ritual was laborious and required a great deal of energy. If he had not purified his system, he would suffer great pain during and after his trance. The pain would last for a few days, as if he had undergone the severest whipping.

While we were preparing for the visit of the Gadong, decorating our family altars, I was holding my son in my arms. He was looking up at me seriously and sighing every now and then. The minute the Gadong entered the room, my son took one look at him and passed away immediately. I asked the Gadong to continue with the *thudam*, even though the child had died.

The oracle was taken to his seat, and two attendants remained with him to support his headdress, which was tied under his chin. The headdress was extraordinary, decorated with peacock's feathers, ceremonial scarves and gold and silver. It was so heavy that two people had to hold it up, or else the oracle would not have been able to raise his head. Over his wide-sleeved *chuba* he wore an elaborate apron. The twenty priests in the room began their prayers in a rhythmic chant, to the music of cymbals and horns, to invite possession of the oracle.

After about ten minutes, the Gadong seemed to feel the effect of the prayers and began to swoon, followed by trembling of his body. Just when he was about to rise from his chair and go into a trance, his face swelled out of all proportion and turned almost purple. Because of this the straps of his headdress tightened and almost strangled him. His attendants immediately loosened the straps so he could breathe.

In his left hand he held an arrow, and in his right a long sword. He stood up and prostrated himself three times to the ground in front of the altar, and began the *cham* dance. He made three turns around the room, shot the arrow into the sky, then threw the arrow away. He waved the sword and people moved away. If he disliked the people around him, he might cut them with his sword. It was a very powerful experience.

After the *cham* dance, he began to speak. A secretary took down what he said, because those unfamiliar with the oracle's language were not able to understand him. After he finished, he collapsed and lay as if death had overtaken him. Immediately his attendants removed his headdress. After some time he revived, moaning loudly in pain and panting, as if all strength had been drained from him. The trance lasted about an hour.

While in trance the Gadong oracle said that

my dead son was a high personage who had made a prayer that, although he was passing away, he would return to his parents. I did not want to accept the oracle's verdict. I said that I was old now, 45, and I did not want to bear another child. I said it would be better for my daughter to give birth to his reincarnation. Before my son died, my daughter had given birth to a daughter. At the time of her birth, my son was gravely ill, but he insisted that he see his niece, so I took him to her. He lifted her hand with great gentleness and caressed it. Three days later he died.

I would always dream of my dead children at regular intervals, but after the death of Tenzing Chota, all such dreams seemed to disappear. We had put his body in a little box within the house, for we were told that he was a sacred person and we should not dispose of his body. I consulted Gonsar Rinpoche, an old lama who often offered prayers in our home, and invited him to do a *thudam*. I asked him to determine the reason for my lack of dreams. I asked him whether it was because we had nailed Tenzing Chota in a box, so his soul had not been able to leave his body.

Gonsar Rinpoche told me that this was decidedly not the case, and that the child had already been reborn. He went on to say that his incarnation was close to me. He said that when a person has been reborn, dreams of that person do not occur. I asked Rinpoche who the incarnation was, if it was one of the workers' children or my newborn granddaughter. He said he did not think so, but that my son had been reborn as a girl. He maintained that this girl would not live very long, and that after her death my son would be reborn as a boy once more.

I persisted that my daughter's child was that new incarnation, but Gonsar Rinpoche did not acknowledge my words. He just said that my daughter's daughter would not live very long, and asked us to be very affectionate towards her. He said that she was too powerful to survive. He also asked us to say prayers for her. A few days later my granddaughter became ill and was ill for seven days. My daughter and her husband decided to take her to Gyatso Shikar, in the hope that she might get better there. For a few days prior to their departure, she had been silent, no crying or tears. But as they were leaving, she screamed as if it tormented her to leave the house. At Gyatso she was deathlike. She lived for three more days.

My husband and I went to Gyatso, where the baby was still struggling to live, in the hope that she would like to see us again. The baby wailed in recognition when my husband arrived, and he fed her a little milk. We called some lamas to say prayers for her, and towards the end of their prayers the baby passed away. While the baby's body was being bathed for burial, we noticed that her entire spinal region was purple. Then we knew that she had broken her spine.

A few days after the death of my granddaughter, I once again began to dream of my own dead son, Tenzing Chota. He was inside a huge cave, naked. I put out my hands and held him close to me. When I told my husband about the dream, he said that the Gadong oracle had predicted that my son would be reborn to me, and that perhaps I was going to conceive again. I rejected this view, as I was unwilling to bear another child.

Despite my misgivings, I gave birth to my son Tendzin Choegyal within the year. Lamas from the monastery of Chomo Lungnga came and told me that their abbot had passed away and that my son was the new incarnation. At about the same time, monks from Drepung monastery also came, saying that my son was a reincarnation of their teacher. I refused to let him go to either place, saying that he was no reincarnation and that I would make him a monk to serve His Holiness.

In time my son developed chronic blisters that would heal and then erupt again. I was told that this was because I had refused to let him take his seat as a *tulku*. Therefore, with great reluctance, I agreed to his going to Chomo Lungnga and becoming Ngari Rinpoche. The Gadong oracle advised me to do so, or else the infant would not live very long. As soon as he went to the monastery, all his illnesses seemed to cease.

He went into Chomo Lungnga monastery when he was three-and-a-half years of age. He remained there for three years, after which he spent three years at Drepung. The monastery of Chomo Lungnga was three hours away from our house. I would often bring him home for a week's holiday, even when he was at Drepung.

My mother was with him when he went to Chomo Lungnga, and how she wept, as he was so very young. I too was very sad to be parted from my youngest son. Later I took him with me to China.

In 1947, one year after the birth of Tendzin Choegyal, my husband died. His death was a crucial test, and I am glad to say that I stood up to it with courage and determination, never letting anyone undermine my spirits, though many in power tried to take advantage of my naiveté and lack of education.

He had gone to visit the Damaka Shikar estate for a day. On his return he was very ill, with severe pains in his abdomen. He lingered for a month, becoming emaciated and terribly weak, after which he died. When he died I saw that blood was coming out of his nose and rectum. The *chang-zo* (manager) of the estate my husband had visited was said to have poisoned him. He was only 48 when he passed away.

At the time of his death, my sons Taktser Rinpoche and Lobsang Samten were both visiting me. It seemed that my husband knew death was imminent, for he asked me to tell the servants to remove the firewood from the *kang*, as he was feeling extraordinarily warm. Then he said he did not want any bedclothes over him, even though it was the first month of the year and very cold. Fifteen minutes later I was summoned back to the room; my husband had passed away. It was midnight.

I quickly had the household awakened, and we all gathered in my husband's room to offer our last prayers to him. Lamas were invited to pray for the departed. My husband was placed in an upright position, with legs crossed and hands folded in the prayer position, as was the custom. He was kept in the house for two days after his death, in keeping with the astrologer's calculations.

In accordance with funeral rites, I removed all jewellery, hair ribbons and even my *hari*. From that day forward, out of respect for my husband, I wore my *hari* only on state occasions, and even then the brocade from the back flap had been removed, as was the custom among Amdo women upon the death of their husbands.

For two days prayers were held in the house, and on the morning of the third day the body was taken away for cremation. The bier was taken to Sangda, three hours away on foot, and it had to be manually carried. My husband's ashes were returned to me, for it had been his explicit wish to have his remains deposited beside the graves of his parents in Tsongkha. He also asked me to see that he did not have a water burial or be fed to birds of prey.

When the ashes were brought to me, I wrapped them in yellow silk and placed them in a little wooden casket in the prayer room. A few months later, when my son Taktser Rinpoche was leaving for Tsongkha, he took this casket with him, carrying it on his back all the way, as it would have been unlucky for anyone else to have touched it. When he arrived at Tsongkha three months later, he conducted prayers for his father at Kumbum, and then he buried the casket close to the graves of my husband's parents.

At Changseshar we held constant prayers for the 49 days of mourning. This is the time ordained for the next rebirth to take form. During the 49 days, it is said that the departed soul remains in his house. The prayers of the last day are the grandest and most elaborate, for rebirth is now taking place. On this day all hair ribbons worn during the mourning are removed and burned, and new clothes, hair ribbons and jewellery are donned. But I did not wear any jewellery for a year.

It was customary that all possessions of the deceased be given away, to lessen the chances of the spirit remaining with the family. In accordance with this, I donated all my husband's clothes, blankets, drinking bowls – everything. Nothing was left as a reminder.

My husband had died leaving my daughter and myself alone at Changseshar. My son Gyalo Thondup was in China at that time, with my son-in-law. Norbu was at Tsongkha.

22

A Political Crisis

In early 1941 the regent, Reting Rinpoche, had taken a leave of absence from his regency, because it was his *ka*, his astrologically evil or unlucky year. He handed the reins of government to Taktra Rinpoche and planned to go on a pilgrimage to India.

Taktra was seventy years of age at the time, and he was a forbidding man. He was one of His Holiness's tutors, and my son was afraid of him. He would whisper to me, 'Amala, Taktra Rinpoche is becoming apprehensive.' He used to carry a silken whip in his hand and on one occasion he struck Lobsang Samten for being too noisy. It was on his authority that Lobsang Samten was not permitted to remain with His Holiness and was sent to school, and then to the monastery with Taktser Rinpoche.

Taktra imposed new regulations on my visits to His Holiness at the Potala. Previously I could go to visit His Holiness whenever I liked, but now Taktra informed us that my daughter and I could not go to see His Holiness so often, and that if we did, one of his men had to accompany us during our visit because he didn't like our private meetings. A meeting was held among the Kashag, the cabinet officials, on his matter. Kashu Kungo (Kashupa) rejected the proposal, saying it was irrational for His Holiness's mother and sister to have someone accompany them during visits. Taktra was so furious that he immediately imprisoned Kashu Kungo.

Mrs Kashu came to me, imploring me to do something for her husband. I therefore wrote to the prison and told them that Kashu Kungo was being held as a result of political intrigue, not because of any wrongdoing. I also appealed for lenient treatment for him. I later heard that my letter had some effect. After His Holiness came of age to rule, and thus the role of Taktra ended, all political prisoners incarcerated during Taktra's rule were released. But during the interregnum, His Holiness had no powers and Taktra, as regent, was the most powerful man in the land.

Reting had asked Taktra to remain regent for three years. It had been agreed between Reting and Taktra that the reins of government would then be handed back to Reting. But at the end of the three years, when Reting tried to take back the regency, Taktra refused to hand back the power, despite the fact that Reting went to see him three times. Reting was so upset that he said he was leaving for Tsongkha, India and China on a pilgrimage. He told us he could not remain in Lhasa, for the times were very bad.

His people and servants pleaded with him to remain. My husband and I also asked him not to leave, and he at last consented.

Generally during your *ka* you break a leg or have some other accident, but Reting's unlucky year began a chain of events that finally proved fatal. A year after he tried to regain power he was imprisoned, and two months after that news arrived that he had died in prison. This was shortly after my husband's death in 1947. Many believed he was assassinated. While Reting was regent, he had had Lungshar's eyes gouged out[1], and Lungshar's son was rumoured to have been behind the death of Reting.

On the night of Reting's death, at about one in the morning, palace guards heard loud cries for help for the direction of the prison. The exact details of his death were never brought to light, but many people were certain he was murdered. Government posters were placed all over Lhasa saying that if anyone speculated that Reting's death had been anything but natural, that person would be severely punished.[2]

[1] Tsipon Lungshar was a lay official, one of the heads of the Revenue Office, who led a movement for reform during Reting's rule.

[2] The Reting-Taktra conflict was, according to historians, not so much a personal power struggle as the focal point for an ongoing political battle between two factions. Taktra's forces were trying to enforce strong central rule over the populace, which some people resisted. The pro-Reting people wanted their power back and sought support from Nationalist China, which sullied their cause in the eyes of many Tibetans. A bomb was sent to Taktra's office during the dispute, and Reting was arrested for masterminding the plot. There followed a rebellion of monks

Our family were close to Reting. Before his arrest, the Kashag tried to recall my son and son-in-law from China. They told me that I should send someone to fetch them back to Lhasa. The Kashag wanted to place all my sons and son-in-law in prison, but they could not do anything, as none of them was in Lhasa. I had also heard that the Kashag wanted to send my daughter and myself back to Tsongkha. Thus they would have been able to disperse the family and eliminate all opposition to their power. What may have forestalled Taktra and his Kashag in their plans was that Ma Pu-fang, the Chinese governor of Amdo, was our friend, and he would have used his power to assist us. Thus they had to think twice about their actions.

Reting Rinpoche and my husband had been very close friends. They had shared a love for horses. The arrest and assassination of Reting would not have been so simple if my husband had been alive, as he had more resources at his disposal than I had, and would at least have prevented the arrest and imprisonment from occurring so smoothly. This is why people are convinced that my husband was poisoned.

loyal to Reting at Sera Monastery, during which the abbot was murdered. The government intervened to put down the rebellion.

The People's Liberation Army took advantage of this chaos and division to make military and political incursions into Tibet. The leadership of the country had been in disarray during the seventeen years of regency, from the death of the thirteenth Dalai Lama until the fourteenth Dalai Lama's assumption of power. In that interim, power struggles raged between competing factions.

At about this time word started to spread that His Holiness was not the real Dalai Lama, that a mistake had been made. It was said that my son was Ditru Rinpoche, while the Ditru Rinpoche was the real Dalai Lama. Ditru Rinpoche was the child of a relative of the thirteenth Dalai Lama. Finally it was decided to place both names in a vessel and, before the image of Je Rinpoche, to shake it and see which name fell out. This would be done three times. My son's name leaped out three times, and the regent Taktra and the Kashag had nothing more to say for themselves. His Holiness was fourteen at the time.

It was such a difficult time. With my sons away and my husband dead, I had never felt so alone and helpless. Tsarong Shape (a *shape* is a cabinet minister) came to see me at about this time and told me to be very cautious, as Tibet was passing through evil hands. He said that what the government thought they were doing, only the gods knew. This was the most troublesome period of my stay in Lhasa, until the Chinese began infiltrating Tibet.

23

A Family Pilgrimage

After my husband died I went on a pilgrimage to Duntse Shikar and Tashilunpo. Our retinue included my youngest daughter Pema, my elder daughter and her two children, Khando and Tenzing Ngawang. The government assisted us by including in our retinue two managers for the pilgrimage – their duty being to see to our lodgings and other comforts.

Duntse was our own property. On this land we had about three hundred *miser* families. The place had been utilised by Je Rinpoche (Tsongkhapa), and it had become a museum. I was afraid in that house. It was very old and seemed to be falling down. The walls were all at a slant. Walking through it took me back aeons in time. Even the furniture was left as it had been during the time of Je Rinpoche, four hundred years ago. There were four enormous prayer rooms, one in each direction. Each prayer room had its own caretaker. Throughout the night ritual drums would resound.

One particular prayer room fascinated me. It had a huge drum with the richest sound I have ever heard, anywhere in Tibet. I was told that if anyone on the property was close to death, this room would be filled with the odour of blood. The place always made my flesh creep, and I was afraid to even walk past it.

After ten days we left for Tashilunpo, head-quarters of the Panchen Lama. It took us three days to get there. At the time of our visit the Panchen Lama was in Tsongkha. We were warm-ly received and stayed in one of the bungalows in the vast gardens. Within the grounds were huge cages for the animals that the Panchen Lama kept, but since he was absent, the cages were empty.

The Panchen Rinpoche at that time was from an Amdo peasant family, like ours. The Tibetan government had selected a boy from Kham, and had made all the preparations for the ceremony. But the Chinese installed their own candidate instead, and sent him to Kumbum to be educated.

At Tashilunpo was a set of clothes that had belonged to Je Rinpoche. It was made of creamy white kidskin – the hat, dress, even the socks were of leather. The dress was scant because, over the years, bits had been broken off by rev-erent worshippers. Tashilunpo also had the *hari* of Je Rinpoche's mother, as they were from Amdo. The *hari* looked so strange to me, far broader, heavier and more cumbersome than modern *haris*.

At Duntse the days had been spent making

offerings at monasteries, and we did the same at Tashilunpo. After ten days there we left and visited smaller monasteries along the way. We then returned to Duntse, where we stayed for three weeks, waiting for my mother and daughter, who were returning to central Tibet from Tsongkha via India.

During my first years in Lhasa I longed to see my mother much more intensely than when we lived in Tsongkha. Every now and then I would send her little gifts that were typical of Lhasa, and she in return would send me little delicacies of Tsongkha that were not available in Lhasa. Only she understood how alone I felt in a strange city.

So when my daughter was travelling to Tsongkha to take a relative of ours back to her family, I asked her to bring back my mother, who was then 73. Shortly after my daughter arrived at Tsongkha, my husband passed away. I sent her a cable to return as soon as she could. Immediately my daughter and mother flew from Tsongkha to China, and then to India. This was the easiest route of travel. I believe that Chiang Kai-shek's wife arranged for an aircraft to take them. From India they came by horseback and met us at Duntse. My mother had to be carried in a palanquin because she was weak and fragile and had broken her arm. I was overjoyed to see her and wept tears of joy. My aunt also came; she was 64. My daughter had been away for two years.

Upon our return to Lhasa, my son Tendzin Choegyal was formally initiated into monkhood, and henceforth became Ngari Rinpoche. An assistant was requisitioned by his monastery to feed and clothe him, and to look after his every need. My brother-in-law Ngawang Changchup came to visit us from Tsongkha at this time via India. He brought me news that he had seen my son, Gyalo Thondup, and that he had two beautiful children. He remained with us for two months and then he had to return to Tsongkha, as responsibilities at Kumbum called him.

24

Communist Occupation

The Chinese had taken over Tsongkha by 1950. Great panic spread through Lhasa, amid rumours that the Chinese were preparing to advance upon us, via Chamdo, which was about to fall to them. At this point His Holiness left Lhasa and set up camp at Dromo (also called Yatung). Prior to our departure for Dromo, a small town about fifteen miles from the border with India and Sikkim, Chinese Communist representatives established themselves in Lhasa, with their wirelesses and transmitters. His Holiness, government officials, aristocrats and my family left for Dromo together.

His Holiness stayed at the monastery of Dungkhar, while my family and I stayed in a nearby monastery. My sons Lobsang Samten and Tendzin Choegyal were with us. My elder daughter was in India for medical treatment, and she had taken her two children and my youngest daughter, Pema, with the intention of placing them in boarding school at Darjeeling. When they heard that we had arrived at Dromo, they came to meet us, and we spent Losar together. Eight months later His Holiness decided to return to Lhasa, as he did not want to remain away from his people too long.[1]

In early 1951 the Kashag insisted that, for his safety, he set up a provisional government at Dungkhar monastery in Dromo. The Tibetan settlements of Kalimpong and Darjeeling in India were just across the border. Before he left he appointed two prime ministers in Lhasa, giving them full authority to run the government, asking that they consult him only in 'matters of the very highest importance'. He planned to return to Lhasa as soon as an agreement had been reached with the Chinese.[2]

After that, I went to India for a pilgrimage, via Nepal. His Holiness suggested that I take my friends Mr and Mrs Taring as my interpreters. They were aristocrats who were with us in

---

[1] Soon after the Communists drove Chiang Kai-shek's Nationalists from mainland China in 1949, they pledged to 'liberate' Tibet. When Tibetan officials sought support from the US, Britain and India, they were turned down. In the autumn of 1950 the Communists attacked eastern Tibet. Soon thereafter, the Nechung and Gadong oracles advised the Dalai Lama to take over the government from the regent Taktra. His Holiness was reluctant, given his youth and the dire situation, but he recognised that the best hope for unification of the country lay with his leadership. He took power in late 1950, at the age of fifteen.
[2] While he was away the government, under threat of violence, signed the Seventeen-Point Agreement with the Chinese. It denied all claims to Tibetan independence but granted regional autonomy. His Holiness returned to Lhasa in August of that year, hoping for the best. He had determined that the only feasible response to Chinese aggression for the outnumbered and ill-prepared Tibetans was non-violence.

Dromo. From Dromo we went to Gangtok, where we left our horses and other animals. At Gangtok we stayed at Yaba Tseten Tashi's residence and another house behind the monastery. After a week's stay we went to Kalimpong by road. There the previous Choegyal of Sikkim treated us with warmth and invited us to dinner. We stayed a month at Kalimpong, preparing for the pilgrimage. We had taken smallpox vaccines, and when we arrived in Nepal my vaccination had swelled out of all proportion, and I was really ill.

We remained a week in Nepal, where the former king invited us as guests to his palace. We had many people with us – Mr and Mrs Taring, Mrs Surkhang, Sadutsang, Ngari Chang-zo, Chang-zo Dakang, as well as servants. The king advised us that it was premature to visit Lumbini, the birthplace of the Buddha, but if we desired to go, he would send an escort of fifty armed guards with us. I refused his good and hospitable gesture, as it would have been a bother for the king, and I thanked him for his consideration.

From Nepal we went to Patna by aircraft, and then by rail to Calcutta, where Gya Lama's daughter was our interpreter. She could not speak Tibetan very well, but she did her best. From Patna we visited Varanasi, Bodi Gaya and other places. After a week we returned to Darjeeling and then Kalimpong. While we were there I decided to return to Tibet, to be with His Holiness. Some Chinese friends asked me whether I wanted to go back to certain death, and told me to remain where I was. Out of fear I did remain at Kalimpong for a year.

While I was there I suffered some sort of paralysis. My daughter went to Gangtok to phone to Dikilingka for a doctor and some medicines. Within six days the medicines arrived. Mrs Panda thought I was at death's door, and she wept a great deal, even giving me Mr Panda's rosary to wear. My youngest son would come to my side and tell me not to go to sleep. When I was sick I wore the rosary, but when I got better he wore it. After two weeks of medical treatment and prayers, I got better.

We then went to Darjeeling for three months. I wrote to my son Gyalo Thondup to come to India, as I was soon planning to leave for Tibet. I had not seen him since his departure for China. Late one night, after I had already retired for the night, I heard the noise of cars driving up the driveway. My servant rushed in to tell me that someone claiming to be my son had arrived. To her he looked like a tall foreigner. Before I could get out of bed, my son was at my side. I had not seen him for many years, and he had changed. He left as little more than a boy, and now he was a man, and a very tall one, too. He had returned with his wife and daughter.

We had sent my son Gyalo Thondup to China at the age of sixteen. I did not want to let him go, as China was so far away, and I was led by a mother's sentiments. But my husband thought it would be a good experience for him. My son was also very keen to go, and as a result there were many household arguments between us. Finally it was decided: Gyalo Thondup would leave for China. I had a premonition that it would be a long while before I would see him again, and my premonition proved to be right. I saw him again only after his marriage in China, when he was about twenty years old.

Gyalo Thondup escorted us back to Lhasa, leaving his family with my daughter. Yaba Tseten Tashi's wife was very considerate when we departed Gangtok. She insisted that I take with me her scarf and gloves, as we were returning in winter and the journey back would be very cold.

When Gyalo Thondup returned with us to Lhasa, he had already decided that Tibet was no longer a safe place and was making plans to leave again. No one knew of this at this time except myself. He did not see eye to eye with the Communists, and in anger some Chinese said that he had to be re-educated. This was an indirect threat, and my son told me that the time would come when the Chinese Communists would try to 'persuade' him to reform his ideas. He pleaded with me to let him go back to India. I reluctantly agreed.[3]

---

[3] By the early 1950s, besides making military advances into eastern Tibet, the Chinese had launched a country-wide campaign of public indoctrination, which included loudspeakers blaring propaganda, interest-free loans to farmers, new hospitals, schools and highways – in an attempt to undermine the monastic system and loyalty to its rule. It was particularly important to the Chinese that the Dalai Lama's family accede to the Communist regime because others, it was assumed, would follow. The takeover was eased by a combination of internal strife, Tibetan isolationism and lack of concern from the rest of the world.

Before he left, Gyalo Thondup made a tour of all our landed property and gave whatever we had in our stores to the *misers*, telling them that they no longer owed us anything. In front of them he burned all the papers that defined their former status. After that he left for India via Duntse, three months after he had come. He chose to leave on the day there was a fair. He begged me not to be angry with him. The only people who knew of his departure were my son Lobsang Samten and myself. We did not inform His Holiness, as Lobsang Samten said that if the Chinese asked His Holiness if he knew the whereabouts of his brother, he would reveal himself by a guilty flush on his face, as he was yet tender in age.

Gyalo Thondup first went to Jayul, to Jora, and then to Tawang. Pemba Rimshi from Dikilingka greatly assisted him by giving him a letter for the Indian border crossing at Tawang. All this secrecy was necessary because, if the Chinese had known of his intended departure, they would not have let him leave Lhasa.

When they arrived at Tawang, the Indian officer was not there. My son and his party were locked up and their guns confiscated. It was only the next day that the government official arrived and gave them a great welcome. My son then told the servants to return to Lhasa, as he was proceeding to India. The servants entreated him to return with them, saying that if he did not, I would be very angry with them. They held on to his legs, asking what they were to tell His Holiness. He told them to tell me that he had dysentery and had to go to India for medical treatment.

By nightfall the servants returned to Lhasa, where they told me that he was not coming back. Though I knew it already, I pretended to fly into a rage and wept a great deal, so that no one would suspect that I knew of the escape plans. I find it very difficult to weep, and do so only under great fear and duress. I told the servants to take the news to His Holiness and to the Chinese officials.

The Chinese were very upset, and they went to His Holiness, who was at Norbulingka. They said they would write to my son to ask him to return. They then came to my residence to comfort me. I was weeping more out of fear than anything else. Later I received word from Pemba Rimshi at Dikilingka that my son had arrived safely in India.

25

A Tour of China

*I*n 1954, when His Holiness was nineteen, the Chinese representatives in Tibet invited him to make a trip to China. He asked me if I would like to accompany him, as he thought it would be a good experience for me, and so I agreed. Before the trip we invited His Holiness to spend a few days in Changseshar, our residence. He had never been to see our home, so it was a great honour for me as well as for the whole household.

We built a new kitchen before he arrived, as well as a new driveway, in the event his car would drive up to the house. Cars had come to Tibet by this time, but never before to Changseshar. We had to prepare food for His Holiness as well as his entire retinue of government officials and the people who waited to seek an audience with him. It was a great responsibility. Prayers were held daily prior to his departure on a long trip. The entire Kashag and many aristocrats were present.

After His Holiness's visit, we made preparations for our departure to China. All our expenses were borne by the Chinese government. The Chinese representatives had asked me to send for my children and grandchildren from India to accompany us on the trip, but I was afraid for their safety, as the Chinese were not what they seemed.[1] I pretended to follow their suggestions and sent my steward to India to see all of them, but I gave secret instructions for them to remain where they were. The Chinese were pleased that I had seemingly acquiesced to their request. I started preparing a wardrobe for the grandchildren, saying that they needed to have the proper clothes to wear in China. The Chinese fairly beamed with delight and pleasure, and once again they told me that I should not allow my family to remain in a foreign land, meaning India.

When my son Gyalo Thondup cabled me, saying that neither he nor the rest of the family would be joining me in China, the Chinese were furious, and did nothing to hide their displeasure. I too had to feign my disappointment in front of them. I gave away the clothes I had prepared to the children of friends.

The people of Lhasa were upset to learn of our departure. They knew that the Chinese were not the gracious hosts they pretended to be, and they greatly feared for our safety. Thinking that they would not see us for a long time, they organised large processions outside our resi-

[1] Living in India at that time were Gyalo Thondup and his wife and children, Jetsun Pema, and Tsering Dolma's children, who were in school.

dence, begging us not to leave. Mass protests were held against the Chinese representatives. People begged the Chinese to see that His Holiness returned to Lhasa after one year.[2]

My daughter Tsering Dolma and my sons Lobsang Samten and Ngari Rinpoche and I left on the first day of the fifth month of 1954. We travelled by horseback from Lhasa to Konken Jinda, then by car for two days, and once again by horseback. The roads were terrible. The Chinese had repaired them in great haste, leaving them filled with rubble. We had to dismount from the horses at many points and travel by foot in order to continue on.[3]

It was an adventurous and dangerous journey. In certain areas we had to cross deep gorges and ravines with planks of wood roughly placed across to make a kind of footpath. In the mountains there was a danger of boulders falling due to prior heavy rains. All of us were put on the alert. Scouting parties would go ahead of us, and if there was any danger they would wave a red flag.

The journey after Konko was very difficult.

[2] The Chinese thought the young, forward-looking Dalai Lama would be favourably impressed by the technological and economic advances he would see in China and might then cooperate in Chinese redevelopment plans for his country. His Holiness decided to accept the invitation, thinking that his attempts at peaceful coexistence might persuade the Chinese to adhere to the Seventeen-Point Agreement. The Tibetan people were afraid his life would be in danger in China, and they were grieved to see him go.
[3] The Chinese had built a new road from Chengdu to Lhasa, but heavy rains had washed away sections of it and brought landslides.

Most of it was done on foot. Our horses were injured from rocks on the road, and many were bleeding. Many of our pack animals fell into the swiftly flowing river while crossing precarious bridges. Seven of them died this way. We did not have proper places to stay at night; temporary bamboo shelters had been erected.

After three days I asked how much more of this we had to endure, as I was of a mind to return to Lhasa. I was told that there were just three more days of this bad road, and then we would meet the cars, as a jeepable road was being prepared. So I continued. My family and I went ahead of His Holiness's party. Our parties numbered three hundred people.

One day as my family, the two tutors of His Holiness and I were travelling, boulders and sediment suddenly began to pour down the hillside ahead of us. After a few hours' wait, I told the two tutors that we should proceed, as the landslide had subsided. The tutors were hesitant, but I decided to move on. My sister-in-law's son was leading a *dri* by the reins, while Ngari Rinpoche had gone on ahead. Suddenly, as we were proceeding, boulders began to tumble down again. My horse stopped immediately at the sound of danger, but my sister-in-law's son's horse, hearing the deadly sound, suddenly leaped fifteen feet. It was a miracle, for if the horse had not leaped, both he and the rider would have been killed. This was the worst moment of our journey.

Two days later we arrived at Shinan, where we stayed for three days. There we met the Panchen

Lama, who continued with us on the journey. My brother-in-law was also there to meet us. After this we arrived at Pochi and remained there for one day. From there we left in powerful Russian jeeps.

It took us two weeks to arrive at the Chinese border from Lhasa. Lanchow, on the border between China and Tibet, is a fertile area with a Mediterranean climate and plentiful fruits. I was struck by the sense of uniformity of the people. Both men and women wore the same type of clothes typical of Communist China – blue shirts and trousers. Even the hats were of blue serge. In Chengdu, Szechwan, we stayed for ten days. I had the feeling that the Chinese were trying to impress us, and we were never taken to any place that would give us adverse opinions. Everywhere we were taken was nice and clean.

From Szechwan we flew to Peking. We had sent our horses and servants back to Lhasa. We stayed three months in Peking, where we were met by Chou En-lai, Liu Shao-Chi, and Chu Teh. We were given a huge three-storey mansion in Peking. His Holiness lived on the top floor with the two tutors, while my family and I lived in the lower floors. On the day we arrived a huge banquet was given to welcome us.

The Chinese overwhelmed us with entertainment. We were never given a moment's rest, and I got very tired. I used to be so thankful when I was back in bed at night. From morning till evening there was some programme, throughout our stay, there was some programme. We would be informed the evening before of the programme for the next day. On some days we had to get up at four in the morning, and we would not return until seven in the evening.

It amused me that a little bell would sound, as a signal that we all had to gather for meals. No matter how delicious the food was, I felt nostalgic for our native food. As soon as the meal was over, a bell would ring again as a sign that we were about to leave for sightseeing. I sometimes pretended to be sick, saying that my arthritis was giving me trouble. But I could not always pretend to be sick, and soon I had to fall in with the Chinese programme once again. Whenever I said I was sick the Chinese doctor would visit me and give me an injection and medicines. The medicines I could get rid of in the toilet, but the injection was unavoidable. Ultimately I decided that sightseeing was the lesser of the two evils.

When His Holiness and the Panchen Lama had their first meeting with Mao Tse-tung, I went too. He had a house surrounded by a lake. He did not look at all impressive to me. He seemed to have some throat problem, for after every few sentences he had to clear his throat. I was taken aback by his house, which was more like a Russian home than a Chinese home. The entire decor and furnishings were of Russian origin. Chou En-lai was more of a statesman than Mao, clever in speech and a subtle diplomat. I was impressed by Madame Soong, wife of the Chinese foreign minister. Though she was in her sixties, there was not a line in her face. I also met Khruschev at this time.

After three months in Peking, we left for

Nanking by train. Snow had fallen and the city looked desolate and bare. We stayed ten days, sightseeing. Then we went to Shanghai, where we celebrated Chinese New Year. Firecrackers burst the whole day. Shanghai was like many other cities in the world, due to so much Western influence. It was also one of the most industrially developed. We could see remnants there of pre-1949 China. There was not so much uniformity in clothing as in Peking, and traces of the old gaiety – of silks and brocades – could be seen. Women were much more fashionable than in ascetic Peking, though there were clear signs that the gaiety was fast coming to an end. In Shanghai I had a sudden urge for hot peppers, and it struck me that when one feels the urge for something, it is never available. I never got my peppers, no matter how hard we looked, and soon I overcame the craving.

Our next stop was Tianjing, where we stayed for four days after two weeks in Shanghai. After this we left for Hangchow, which was covered with newly fallen snow. Hangchow is the centre of the silk industry. After ten days there we went to Wuxi. From Wuxi we travelled to Yenna, to Xian and then to Dalian, a major industrial city. With so many factories, the entire city was clogged with pollution and smoke. On each day of our stay there, we saw practically all the factories.

We spent six days in Yampel, close to the Korean border. The dialect and clothing there were a little different from the rest of China. They wore their traditional styles of dress, with very broad sleeves. They are a very tall people. Passing through the countryside, we saw peasant women carrying all their baggage on their heads, as in the Indian countryside.

We spent Tibetan Losar back in Peking. Since we were in a foreign country, we had a much simplified New Year. In the morning we honoured His Holiness, and then the Chinese entertained us with their opera for the rest of the day.

I was struck by the poverty in the Chinese countryside. We were never taken to see poor areas, but sometimes it was unavoidable. People lived in little bamboo huts with no furnishings at all. Sometimes when we got out of the car, these peasants would furtively put out their hands, asking for a donation. Equally furtively, I would put some money in their hands, and quietly they would appeal to me to not say a word, or they would be severely punished. One of the peasants told me that if the government knew he was begging, he would be killed forthwith. We saw empty coffins strewn along the road; they had been robbed by poor people. Since the peasants did not have animals, the ploughs were pulled by humans.

I did quite a lot of shopping in China for fabrics and silks. All the good brocades available during the Kuomintang were gone, and we found only silks of inferior quality. All expenses were paid for by the Chinese. For the year that we were away, the Chinese gave me about a thousand *tayuan* per month. The others received between seven hundred and a thousand. Later they gave us ration cards instead of money. They made us summer and winter clothes in the Tibetan style. The Chinese were obviously trying to bribe us.

In the stores there was a limit to what one could buy. Once when I was refused access to more than the quota of fabric, my interpreter hastily told the clerk that I was the Dalai Lama's mother, and only then was I permitted to buy what I chose. All the stores took ration coupons rather than money.

Some of the places we saw in China were pleasant, but their beauty was lost on me because we had to do what the Chinese wanted us to do. We did not have time to enjoy the place quietly. Never have I longed more for Tibet than during those days in China. I really got no pleasure out of the trip, even though the Chinese tried to be good hosts. The only thing I enjoyed in China was the opera.

It was compulsory for the Chinese staff in the evenings to listen to the radio or political announcements. I knew this because the girl who assisted me had to go every evening. On Saturdays, she would rush to wash her hair, as she had so little free time. The first Chinese girl who assisted me got married. Thirteen days after her marriage, her husband was sent to Lanchow; this was the Chinese system. Because she was visibly pregnant a few months later, she was dismissed from her duties as my assistant.

She wept a great deal when she departed, and said that misfortune had befallen China. She told me I was lucky to be able to return to Tibet, but warned me that misfortune would also befall

Tibet. Later, when we left for Tibet, all the Chinese staff wept and begged us to take them back with us. They began crying ten days before our departure. Even Chou En-lai was weeping as he bade us farewell. Life must indeed have been difficult in Communist China, or else they would not have wept like that.

We flew from Peking to Lanchow and then took the train to Amdo, which the Chinese call Chinghai. We stayed five days at Kumbum monastery, where great ceremonies were held. Then we went to Taktser, driving by car for two hours, and then riding horses since there was no motorable road after this. I heard that the people of Tsongkha had been compelled to make the roads for his Holiness's visit, but when we passed there, the people had been sent away and were not permitted to meet him.

Tsongkha had become wretched. We saw signs of poverty everywhere; peasants wore tattered clothes and lived in a scene of total destitution. Most of them could not even speak, but remained miserably silent. When people came to see us at Taktser, eight or nine soldiers maintained watch at the door, and within the audience room one soldier listened to our conversations. It therefore was very difficult for visitors to speak at will. Before visitors were allowed to see me, they underwent strict interrogation as to the purpose of their visit. If they did not keep their conversation within strict limits they would be punished. Even their time was limited.

When they entered the room, I would ask them how they were. Their immediate reply would be, 'By the courtesy of Chairman Mao, we are very happy.' And so saying, they would weep, tears flowing as from a tap. When they left the room they were once more interrogated as to the content of their conversation. Even my relatives could not speak; all they did was weep in sorrow.

Every monastery had supplies that could last them for many years, kept in special storerooms. The Chinese had ransacked these and removed everything at Kumbum. All the land of the monastery had been usurped by the Chinese, and I saw that the monastery could no longer support itself.

I went back to my old home. The house had been taken down and a new one had been built. It had been my husband's dream that we would all go back to Tsongkha and retire. He often told me that, since our family had steadily expanded, there would not be enough room in the old house, so he had asked the monastery of Takster to supervise the building of a new house. This was the first time I saw it. I was glad that my husband was not there to see that his dream would never be fulfilled. It was three times the size of our old home; there were rooms for all of us.

After our stay at Takster we returned to Tsongkha and stayed three days. We returned back to Lhasa by way of China. In Lanchow, which was very similar to Tsongkha, we passed roadside inns where I could see food for sale that was similar to our food in Tsongkha. I yearned to have some, and since the Chinese did not permit us to eat from inns without a doctor's certificate, I quietly sent one of our servants to buy food from the restaurants and conceal it in his *chuba*. We all enjoyed the food secretly in our rooms.

From Lanchow we went by ship for six days to Hanchow. After two days the ship had to be halted, as the seas were rough and there was a danger that we might strike the formidable rocks. The ship was very large, holding three hundred people, and we enjoyed ourselves very much. From Hanchow we went to Kunming, which was on a hill, and stayed for three days. Leaving Szechwan, we were held up for ten days, as the route ahead of us had suffered a severe earthquake and the roads were damaged.

Our trip to China had been a good but tiring experience. His Holiness even learned about two thousand Chinese characters during that year. It amused me to see that he would participate in the Chinese exercises in the early morning. Even my son and son-in-law would join in, because the Chinese made it compulsory for all the men.

Ngari Rinpoche was five at the time, and the Chinese really spoiled him, taking him with them everywhere. In fact, we never spoke against the Chinese in front of him, as we were afraid that he would repeat it innocently to them, as he was so young. Because we stayed in China for so long, the Chinese who accompanied us became almost fluent in Tibetan. We already knew some Chinese, and our hosts would flatter me, saying that I could speak the colloquial language well.

We arrived back in Lhasa on the first day of the fifth month, exactly one year after our departure. The people came out to meet and welcome us, thronging the roadsides for the last two hours into Lhasa. I had gone a day ahead of His Holiness's party, as my mother was not well. His Holiness went straight to Norbulingka, where there was a welcoming ceremony.

We were amazed and frightened by the increase in the numbers of Chinese in Lhasa. We heard rumours that the Chinese were preparing to take over Tibet soon. Before we left China, Mao had told His Holiness that the fate of Tibet was in His Holiness's hands. Mao asked him to redistribute the land among all the people within the next year or two. His Holiness said it would be wiser to change the system gradually.

Lobsang Samten had been appointed head of His Holiness's household and treasury, but he got very sick and had to leave his post. He was delirious for two days and nights, and would beat anyone who came near him. The doctor told me that he would have to undergo a treatment. I readily agreed. Pulverised garlic was placed on his chest, then lighted incense was placed over it. Four men held my son down while the heat from the incense reached his flesh. A huge blister formed and erupted. This same treatment was conducted on both shoulders and below the nape of the neck. Afterwards my son was like a corpse. A spoon had to be used to unclench his teeth so that medicine could be given to him. After two days of delirium, he gradually recovered.

The doctor who saw to my son was famous in Lhasa. He could diagnose my illness just by feeling my shoe or belt. I did not have to go in person; I would just send him an article of my clothing. But he would never attend to people if they were past the age of fifty; he said it was a waste of time, as they were about to die. To this day I regret that we did not bring him with us when we escaped from Tibet in 1959. The day before I left Lhasa, I had asked him to bring me a large quantity of medicines, and he did so. He was staying at Changseshar, so I could not tell him we were going, as the servants might have got wind of our plans.

26

Buddha's Birthday

*I*n 1956 we went on a pilgrimage to India with His Holiness. This was the Buddha Jayanti year. (The Buddha's birthday celebration that year was the 2,500th.) We left in the ninth month, with thousands of other Tibetans. We went by car to Gangtok. It took five days. His Holiness went straight from Gangtok to Bombay by plane. My family and I went to Calcutta. Gyalo Thondup and Tsering Doma went by plane from Calcutta to Bombay, Varanasi and Bodh Gaya.

Later we went to Kalimpong where we stayed at Raja Dorje's home. The thirteenth Dalai Lama had stayed there once. During a one-month pilgrimage we went to all the big cities and made a tour of south India by train. It was in south India that my son Samten had an operation for appendicitis, and my nephew had his tonsils removed at Bhakra Nangal. Every three to four days I would make our native food. His Holiness and the two tutors really enjoyed it, since we had Indian food most of the time. We would eat it sitting on the bed.[1]

Upon our return to Tibet, the Chinese had become very powerful. They had issued orders to bring back my sons. I was so worried I could not eat or sleep. My son-in-law and daughter had to attend Communist propaganda meetings, carry stones to make roads and till the land. The Chinese took everything they wanted from us, and they even started to cut down our trees. All the aristocrats had to perform labour, even Madame Ragashar. She used to tell me she would refuse to go, even at the price of death. But later she was forced to go, as part of the women's association.[2]

The Chinese came to Changseshar and told me it would be a good idea to convert the place into government offices. I told them to take it, as I was alone and did not need such a large place. They wanted to pay me cash, but I refused. They said that if I did not accept money, people would later say that they had robbed me. They even said they would bring electricity to the house. They would send me gifts and try to win me over. They told me that,

[1] His Holiness had gone to India in part to seek support for the Tibetan cause from Prime Minister Nehru, but help was not forthcoming. The family urged His Holiness to consider staying in India, but he felt he needed to be with his people in their time of need. He returned to Lhasa in early 1957. Diki Tsering stayed behind until August 1958, with Norbu and Lobsang Samten. Gyalo Thondup was already living in India.
[2] By this time the Chinese Communists had dropped all pretence of non-violence in Tibet. As armed occupation spread, so did resistance, some of it with CIA backing.

with my children away, they would look after me, that I could go to Kalimpong for a vacation during the winters and reside in a house they had bought there, and that I could spend my summers in Lhasa. They would foot all the expenses. They claimed that their territory extended all the way to Siliguri, which is just south of Kalimpong. I had nothing to say.

They would drop in any time they wanted. Whenever they told me they were coming, I would feel nervous, wondering what they would talk about. When they left I would feel light, and heave a sigh of relief. I was so afraid. I had to be very careful what I said, or else I might hurt some other party through careless words.

I was harassed to attend meetings, dinners, movies and so on. I never went, despite the fact that they insisted. This brought me into disfavour with the Chinese. I made the excuse either that I had disliked amusements from a tender age or that I was sick. When I refused to see movies on the pretext that I had weak eyesight, they even brought a projector to Changseshar to show me the films. They insisted that I attend their meetings. I told them that this was quite useless, as I did not know how to read or write. I told them that, if they wished, I would clean their rooms and offices and do their laundry. I also told them, sardonically, that it was pointless to invite me, as I would only occupy an extra chair and drink their tea. After that they left me alone.

27

Escape into Exile

Gradually life in Lhasa became un-
bearable, and we began to think
about escape. Our decision to leave
took place around the eighth or ninth
month of 1958. I was living at Changseshar with
my mother. My daughter and son-in-law resided
close by in the commander-in-chief's residence.

For months my daughter and I had been talk-
ing late into the night about means of escape. It
amuses me now when I recall the many foolish
plans we made. Once my daughter suggested
that both of us travel as nuns with shaven heads.
I did not think it feasible, but she thought it
might work if we said we were going on a pilgrimage. She even suggested that we put black
paint on our faces, so people would not recognise us. Finally His Holiness told us that these
plans were not possible, and that we must plan
everything carefully so that we would not be
caught. He told us to wait for a while, as the time
was not ripe for escape.

In the meantime, the Karmapa's sister sent

word to me that her brother was planning to escape and asked me to inform His Holiness. (His Holiness the Karmapa is head of the Kagyu school, one of the four schools of Tibetan Buddhism.) He had sent all his belongings to Bhutan, and he was leaving soon as the Chinese were harassing him. The Karmapa's monastery was built on a hill, and the Chinese had opened fire on it, making it impossible for him to remain there. His sister also asked me on behalf of the Karmapa to beseech His Holiness to leave Tibet. She asked us all to go with her brother and her to India.

I replied that so long as His Holiness was still in Tibet, I could not leave. I told her that we were planning to go, though we did not know when, and that I would convey her message to His Holiness. This happened in the eleventh month. In the meantime, His Holiness was consulting his state oracles. They kept saying that the time was not yet right. Finally they told His Holiness that 19 March would be a good time to leave, between nine and eleven at night.

On 10 March I was at Changseshar, doing my knitting and embroidery and supervising the dyeing of materials. An Amdo friend came and asked me why I was still doing such things. Did I not know there was an uprising going on? His Holiness had been invited to a function at the Chinese Military Command and saw no option but to accept. The people of Lhasa had staged a mass sit-in around Norbulinkga to prevent him from leaving. People had armed themselves, and those without arms had even taken up pitchforks. My *chang-zo*, the house manager, did not know of the uprising either, and was still doing his accounts.[1]

My Amdo friend told me that I had to leave for Norbulingka immediately. My *chang-zo* tried to find out what was happening. He said he would have to bolt all the gates and doors, as the people would pour into Changseshar. The area surrounding Norbulingka was in chaos, and people were shouting, begging His Holiness not to leave. They said that he would be allowed to pass only over their dead bodies. No Communist personnel or cars were permitted near Norbulingka. If they did come near the mob, they were stoned and beaten. My son-in- law had sent a car for me and since the driver, Lhakpa, had on a Chinese uniform, he was beaten and almost stoned to death. Finally one of the mob recognised him and brought a halt to the violence.

My son-in-law came to escort my daughter and me to Norbulingka. The roads were barricaded by Khampa warriors, to prevent a Chinese intrusion. Even my daughter and son-in-law had to obtain a permit from army personnel in order to escort me, or else they would not have been let through the crowds. When they came, they told me I had to leave immediately. I did

[1] The Chinese had insisted that His Holiness attend a theatrical performance, and that he come alone, without his usual body-guards, setting off fears of a kidnapping attempt. Thousands of people gathered outside Norbulingka, where he was in residence, to prevent him from going. The crowd grew to thirty thousand. It was a turning point in the strained relations with the Communists.

not even have time to pack anything. I did not know that it was the last I would see of Changseshar and my mother.

I heard that, early that same day, the Chinese had picked up my son Tendzin Choegyal from Drepung to attend a function at their military headquarters. They had also come to pick me up at Changseshar, while I was still there. They came into the house armed, eight men and four women. When they tried to enter my personal chambers, my *chang-zo* pushed them violently away. He told them I was not well. After a look of hatred, they left the same way they had come.

I was so worried for Tendzin Choegyal. I thought they would now hold him in custody, since His Holiness and myself had not attended their function. All day I heard him calling 'Amala, Amala', as if he was suffering. I sent scouts to look into their offices, but all they could see was a Chinese official making a violent speech, banging on the table. Many aristocrats were there, but there was no sign of my son. We thought they would take him to China. But, to our surprise, at nightfall they escorted him back to Drepung. He was intercepted on the way by his *chang-zo*, who brought him back to us.

So we were all safe in Norbulingka. No one was permitted to enter, and there was no communication with the Chinese. I heard that there were street fights and many people were killed. Chensalinka monastery was fired upon by the Chinese, and seven monks were killed at Drepung. During this time the Khampa soldiers had taken control of all the small boats, so our departure would be simplified. If they had not done this we would not have been able to leave, for every road had been taken over by the Chinese.

Our employees would come every morning from Changseshar to bring milk, bread and other provisions. Each employee had to have a yellow badge, given by the people, or they would not have been permitted entry. People kept watch outside Norbulingka throughout this period. I had locked everything in Changseshar and left the keys wrapped in silk, with a note attached for my *chang-zo*. This note probably saved his life after we left Lhasa. The Chinese questioned him about our escape, not believing that he did not know of our plans. They were about to torture him when he produced my note, telling him to take charge of the house and that I was placing the keys in his custody. I also told him that I was leaving, but that I did not know where I was going.

We did not tell my mother we were going. This was very sad for me, but I knew that at 87 she could not travel on horseback. We had been staying at Norbulingka, and she was at Changseshar. She hated the Communists and always gave them scoldings. She thought it unjust that they took her property, which she and her husband had built with effort and labour.

I could not even get my clothes from Changseshar, for if I had done so the servants would have become suspicious. I tried to send a young girl to Changseshar to fetch a heavy fur coat for my journey, but at the gates of

Norbulingka she was so severely questioned about the purpose of her errand that she had to turn back. Two days before our departure our horses were taken to Ramaka, on the other side of the river, on the pretext that they were going to get manure. Our meagre belongings and food supplies were also sent with this caravan.

My daughter and I were the first party to leave Norbulingka on 19 March, both of us disguised as soldiers. I borrowed my son-in-law's short fur dress so I would look like a man. We obtained men's boots and scrubbed them with mud to give them an old look. Even my hat was borrowed from one of the servants. Over my shoulder I slung a little toy rifle, which would have looked ridiculous during the day but was not noticeable at night. My daughter was also dressed like a man, and my son was dressed as a soldier. On the 18th we sat up all night to sew him a fur dress for the journey.

At eight forty-five we left from a side gate. His Holiness followed fifteen minutes later, followed by his two tutors and members of the Kashag. His Holiness was also dressed as a soldier. He walked behind my son-in-law as his servant. Though we were surrounded by Communists, fortune smiled on us that night. The mist was heavy, so we could slip out undetected. It seemed as if the gods had closed the ears, eyes and minds of the Chinese and assisted us through the ordeal. As we passed the Chinese headquarters, it was filled with bright lights; they were still in their offices, working and conducting meetings.

We crossed the river Tsangpo in skin boats and waited on the other side for His Holiness and his party. Our horses were there. There were a hundred of us, and the sound of the horses along the gravel sounded like thunder. I kept praying and telling the others to make as little sound as possible. It was a miracle that the Chinese did not hear the sounds of horses at a trot.

After crossing the Tsangpo we were so afraid that the Chinese would miss us that we started to move at a gallop, and that did make quite a noise. But they apparently did not know of our departure until the 22nd, three days after our escape. They shelled the Norbulingka on that day, and only then did they gain entry. After one look around they knew that His Holiness had left. They looked for him in Chinsalinka, and then at Chomolungo and Drepung.

Much blood was shed in Lhasa in the aftermath of our escape. One of our employees who left after we did told me that when he was leaving Lhasa it seemed as if he was walking over fields of dried peas. There were empty rifle cartridges, for miles around.

We had been instructed by the Kashag not to take anything with us, so we had not even taken any food supplies. Now we saw that many of the others had brought a lot of their belongings and food, too. The only thing I brought was a woollen blanket, which served me well on the journey, and a little *tsampa*.

We had crossed the Tsangpo at midnight. From midnight until the next day at nine o'clock we rode non-stop and at great speed. I had no scarf or glasses and, since I had on a short man's dress, I froze on the way. When we stopped at Chitsusho I could barely stand from a mixture of cold, fatigue and cramps in my legs. It had been very windy, and thick dust caked my face. It was a week before I could wash my face. My skin began to peel because I had no protection against the wind and dust storms.

The *misers* and peasants along the way were so good to us, bringing us food supplies and whatever they could afford. It was very touching. They would even bring us shoes and sweaters, weeping with sorrow at the fate of Tibet. We travelled in two parties. One party would go ahead, and when the second party caught up, the first would go ahead again.

There were about two hundred armed Khampas escorting us.[2] If it had not been for them, we would have made many wrong turns. We did mistake some roads and had to return again, thus wasting valuable time. Once, far in the distance, we saw horses approaching. We panicked and thought instantly of the Chinese but, to our relief, it was a group of Khampa soldiers coming to look for us. We told them that His Holiness was due to arrive soon. We were a day ahead of him at that point.

When we arrived at Tsonadzong, we heard the roar of aircraft engines. Once again we thought

---

[2] The warriors from Kham were known for their horsemanship and fierce resistance to the Chinese occupation. They were enlisted to protect the Dalai Lama and his party on their journey to India.

the worst. All of us quickly dismounted and laid ourselves flat on the ground. My daughter shouted to me to lie beneath my horse. The aircraft passed overhead and continued on its way. It was about ten in the morning and had been snowing. We heard later that it was a plane sent by the Indian government to see if they could spot us.

His Holiness was delayed along the way by people seeking audiences. Many people left for India as soon as His Holiness did. Most people did not know we were leaving, as we were passing at night and could not be seen. When we arrived at Sanda, I could barely stand, I was so cold. Villagers invited us into their house, but we did not have time.

We arrived at Chidisho via Ramaka and Sanda. This place was famous in Tibet for its handwoven woollens. His Holiness laughed when he saw me, as I was still dressed like a man. He said that I must have had a difficult time, but that it was all for the best – that the ordeal would soon be at an end. We spent the night here, and since there was no proper place to stay, we slept in a loft above the pigs. I changed my dress here. When we spent a night somewhere, I would always bake bread for the next day's journey. We survived on *tsampa* and *thukpa*.

We were a bit more relaxed after Chidisho. We had left the Chinese far behind. The Khampa soldiers had gone ahead to clear the way for us, shooting any Chinese that they came upon. At Yarto Takla, many local oracles came to

call; they went into a trance, saying there would
be no danger and that our journey to India was
clear.

28

Safe Haven in India

There was a big reception at Tawang, just over the border, where we were met by Indian officials. No one in India had known we were leaving Lhasa, except for my son Gyalo Thondup, who was in touch with the Khampas. At Tawang the Indian official knew how to speak a little Chinese and would repeat *hang-hao*, (very good), whenever he was given some of the bread I had baked. After three days at Tawang, we went to Bomdila. After Bomdila we went to Tezpur, where we were met by Gyalo Thondup and government officials, including Nehru. His Holiness gave sermons there. Then we went to Siliguri, where we were greeted by many Tibetans. When I met my daughter and grandchildren, I couldn't say anything; only tears came.

At Mussoorie we were given a great reception. The Indian guards and army provided security, and it was a relief to be safe. The government looked after our every need and was very kind to us. We had privacy and peace there, as the

Chinese were far away and did not give me any cause for panic, as they had during the last few years in Lhasa. We went for walks in the huge gardens and saw movies. In those days, coffee was my favourite at the restaurants, something I never had in Lhasa. But I disliked the rickshaws, as I did not like the idea of men pulling them. Mussoorie was full of Tibetans and we stayed there for a year. His Holiness held press conferences and spoke to many people about the situation in Tibet.

We were then moved to Dharamsala, where we stayed at Swargashram. The building used to leak a lot. When I was still in China, I had had X-rays taken and had been told that I had a pouch-like growth in my throat, in which food particles would collect. They said it required an operation, but they would not operate on me as I was advanced in age. Because it had never given me any problem, I did not believe them. When I returned to Lhasa, at a dinner for the Chinese I suddenly felt as if something was stuck in my throat. From that time on I had trouble with my throat. In Mussoorie I had great difficulty eating. My condition steadily grew worse in Dharamsala.

Finally His Holiness advised me to go abroad for medical treatment. I did not want to go, as I thought I would die from an operation. My son Norbu then took me to Calcutta to consult a doctor. He gave the same diagnosis I had been given in China, and said it was necessary to have an operation. An English doctor there said he would operate on me if I went to England. He said I had a rare disease, afflicting one in every ten thousand people. So I returned to Dharamsala to take my leave of His Holiness. On my way I was in a motor accident, resulting from a tyre puncture. I suffered injuries and lost consciousness for an hour.

I was like a child after my accident. I could not put on my clothes or even eat without the assistance of a maid. After ten days I left for England, accompanied by my son Norbu and Mrs Taring. She acted as my interpreter for the visit. I went into hospital immediately. For the first ten days I received treatment for injuries sustained in the accident, after which I had my operation. A week later I left the hospital. Norbu had left ten days after our arrival in England.

Lady Gould, whose husband had been stationed in Lhasa with the British mission, was kind to me during this period. She often visited and took me sightseeing. I stayed near the sea in a hotel for three months with Mrs Taring. Mrs Taring was good to me, though I am sure she must have had a difficult time. Sometimes I would get up at night feeling nostalgic for Tibetan food, and Mrs Taring would cook for me in the hotel kitchen. After a few amusing mistakes, she could soon cook well. I was fascinated by the gas stove, which I had never seen in Tibet. The hotel staff treated us like family members, and we would often cook for them, which they enjoyed.

One day we were visited by the police, who told us that some robbers were on the prowl.

Mrs Taring was so afraid that she began to throw our handbags under the bed. I told her that if a thief were to enter the room, the first thing he would see were the handbags under the bed.

We were sad to leave the seaside hotel, which had become home for three months. Gyalo Thondup came to visit me during this period, and then took me on a tour of America, Japan and Hong Kong. His wife came too. When we arrived in America, I was told that my mother had passed away. We stayed three weeks in New York, then went to Washington, San Francisco, Japan and Hong Kong, before returning to India. I was away for four-and-a-half months.

When we returned to Dharamsala, my daughter was very sick. Her illness had begun two years before my departure for England. She had been put in charge of the Nursery for Tibetan Children at Dharamsala. At the time we did not suspect cancer, but she always had pain in the stomach. She went to Calcutta for treatment for two months, and I went with her. Finally she was taken to England for her treatment.

Ten days after her arrival in England, she passed away in hospital. I had a peculiar dream on the night she died. In my dream I saw beggars outside our residence in Dharamsala wearing Tibetan dresses that were loosely draped, not tied up with belts. In their midst was my daughter, eating with them. 'What is she doing there?' I thought angrily. Then I woke with a start. She had been wearing a blue dress hanging loosely about her. I had a premonition that she had died.

We received the telegram three hours later. When my son-in-law returned from England, I asked him what my daughter was wearing at her death. He replied that he had put a blue brocade dress on her, minutes before her death, loosely wrapped around her. She was cremated there and we had prayers said for her.

In her final years, Diki Tsering continued to look after her family, especially her youngest son, Tendzin Choegyal. She saw that he got a good education, at St. Joseph's College in Darjeeling. In the end he gave up his vows, finding it impossible to reconcile his modern acculturation with the expectations of monastic life. He now runs a guesthouse in Dharamsala.

In 1960 Norbu took up a teaching post at the University of Washington in Seattle. There he decided to give up his monastic vows to marry. He is now retired from a professorship at the University of Indiana. He has written two books, Tibet Is My Country *and* Tibet. *Lobsang Samten also married, and he ran the Tibetan Medical Centre until his death in 1985.*

Tsering Dolma was head of the Tibetan Children's Village, a nursery for orphaned and destitute children, until her death, at which time Jetsun Pema took it over. Pema has written an autobiography, Tibet, My Story, *published in 1997.*

Gyalo Thondup, a powerful political force on the Tibetan refugee scene and a successful businessman with international connections, continued to gather support around the world for the Tibetan cause until his retirement.

Diki Tsering's health was not good in her last years.

In 1980 her sister came from Tibet for a visit, bringing dreadful news about events and conditions back home. Those close to her said that she never recovered from the loss of heart that resulted from hearing about the destruction of the people and places she so loved.

That winter she died at her home, Kashmir Cottage, in Dharamsala. Her son Lobsang Samten and Tendzin Choegyal's wife, Rinchen, were with her. When His Holiness visited her for the last time, he told her not be afraid, and she told him she was not. He told her to meditate on the sacred thangka painting on her wall and say her prayers. At the end she wanted to sit up, and she passed away in meditation. Her only regret was that the rest of her family were not present. The whole family gathered to mourn for her. She was cremated in Dharamsala, and prayers were said for her by Tibetans everywhere.

Afterword

*Y*ou could say my grandmother's life was colourful, but you could also say it was plain. One of her most enduring gifts to all of us was a very humble one – *thukpa tientu* (pulled noodles). It was a common dish in Amdo and she made it often for her family. Then she taught my father to make it, he taught me, and I taught my daughter.

You cut up mutton and steam it with a little pepper and salt. You have to cook it until it's chewy, but not too chewy. If it got too soft, we'd get a scolding. I had endless problems getting it right. Then fresh dough is kneaded with a little oil, and it's pulled off into small flat noodles, which are thrown into the boiling soup. You put the lid on, and on the first boil you take it off, or the dough will get too soft. The timing is important.

Grandmother introduced this soup into the refugee community in India and its popularity spread, until now its the closest thing we have to a Tibetan national dish. Everyone makes it. I think she would be pleased that her food continues to nourish thousands of Tibetans every day.

Of course, her greatest contribution, not only to the Tibetan people but to the world, was giving birth to three incarnate lamas, including the child who became the fourteenth Dalai Lama. His vision and exemplary leadership have served the cause of human dignity and world peace for fifty years.

When his mother died, His Holiness announced her passing to a gathering of devotees under the bodhi tree at Bodh Gaya. He described what a virtuous life she had led and how many *manis* (recitations of the mantra '*Om mani padme hum*') she had said in her final years. He was not sad, he said, because he was confident that she would have a good rebirth. I am sure she is back with us now, bringing comfort to everyone around her with her indomitable spirit.

Glossary

amala mother

Amdo Area populated mainly by Tibetans but then ruled by Muslim warlords in the name of Nationalist China; frontier land with uncertain borders. Wild, windswept, high mountains, grassland, forests, salt lakes. China called it Chinghai, claimed it as its own. Populated first by Tibetans, then later Chinese and Chinese Muslims moved in. Since eighteenth century rules by kings and warlords often supported by China.

chang beer made from barley

Changseshar 'Eastern Garden'; house where family lived in Lhasa; also called *chensi-sha*

chang-zo corresponding secretary; manager

Choekyong Tsering Dalai Lama's father

Chokah Jorkha, Churkha, twenty-two kilometres from Taktser, birthplace of Sonam Tsomo

chuba belted dress worn by both men and women

damaru small ceremonial drum

Darjeeling Indian city in Himalayas; its name is a corruption of the Tibetan 'Dorji Ling' ('Place of the Thunderbolt')

Diki Tsering ('Ocean of Luck'), name given to Dalai Lama's mother by Taktser Rinpoche when she was a new bride

domadesi a kind of pastry

Doma Yangzom Diki Tsering's mother

Drepung large monastery

dri female yak

dzo male cross between yak and cow

Gadong oracle state oracle

Ganden large monastery

Guyahu Tanantwan, where Diki Tsering's grandfather bought farm

Gyayum Chenmo 'Great Mother', people called Diki Tsering by this name

hari vase-shaped headdress studded with jewels, reaching to the waist

Je Rinpoche Tsongkhapa, founder of the Gelugpa sect

Kalimpong in far northern Bengal, a traditional trading centre between Tibet and India

kang a heated platform used for sitting and sleeping

Kashag Dalai Lama's inner cabinet, Council of Ministers

Kumbum market town close to Taktser; also the monastery

kyirong ghost

labrang religious corporation

Lha gyal lo 'Victory to the Gods'

lhamo Tibetan opera

Losar Tibetan New Year

Ma Pu-fan Chinese warlord of Chinghai province

miser bonded labourers

Monlam Great Prayer Festival, during Losar

Namgyal monastery in Potala

Nechung state oracle

ngagpa priest

Ngari Rinpoche youngest son of Diki Tsering – born Tendzin Choegyal

Ngawang Chnagchuup Choekyang Tsering's brother, senior steward of Kumbum

Norbu, Thubten Jigme twenty-fourth incarnation of fifteenth-century monk and teacher Taktser

Norbulingka ('Jewel Park'), summer home of Dalai Lama

nyerpa servant in charge of household stores

pangden apron worn by ladies of Lhasa

patu headdress worn by ladies of Lhasa

Potala Palace home of Dalai Lama; contains Namgyal monastery and government offices

Reting regent; Dalai Lama's senior tutor

Sera large monastery

shape cabinet minister

Sonam Tsomo Diki Tsering's original name

Taktra Rinpoche regent; also Dalai Lama's tutor

Taktser Ta-tse, Ji-ga-chuan Hunn-ne, ('Roaring Tiger'); at nine thousand feet altitude, one of six villages under jurisdiction of Kumbum monastery; about thirty smallholdings on a hillside

Taktser Rinpoche previous one died shortly

before birth of Tsering Dolma; son Norbu was next incarnation

Tashi deleg   New Year's greeting

Tashi Dhondup   Diki Tsering's father

thangka   religious paintings on cloth scrolls

thudam   divination

thukpa   noodles in broth, from Amdo. In Lhasa it was made a national dish by Diki Tsering

timomo   steamed dumplings

tsampa   roasted barley meal

Tsongkha   district in Amdo; birthplace of Tsongkhapa

tulka   incarnate lama, addressed as Rinpoche ('Precious One')

yuleg   servants employed on yearly basis